IN OUR WORDS

Yenn Purkis and Wayne Herbert

IN OUR WORDS

Stories from the Intersection of LGBTQIA+ Identity and Disability

Foreword by Philippa Moss

The Disability Studies Collection

Collection Editors

Dr Damian Mellifont

& Dr Jennifer Smith-Merry

LPp

First published in 2024 by Lived Places Publishing.

The authors and editors have made every effort to ensure the accuracy of information contained in this publication, but assume no responsibility for any errors, inaccuracies, inconsistencies, and omissions. Likewise, every effort has been made to contact copyright holders. If any copyright material has been reproduced unwittingly and without permission the Publisher will gladly receive information enabling them to rectify any error or omission in subsequent editions.

British Library Cataloguing in Publication Data
A CIP record for this book is available from the British Library

ISBN: 9781915734532 (pbk)
ISBN: 9781915734556 (ePDF)
ISBN: 9781915734549 (ePUB)

The right of Yenn Purkis and Wayne Herbert to be identified as the Authors of this work have been asserted by them in accordance with the Copyright, Design and Patents Act 1988.

Cover design by Fiachra McCarthy
Book design by Rachel Trolove of Twin Trail Design
Typeset by Newgen Publishing UK

Lived Places Publishing
Long Island
New York 11789

www.livedplacespublishing.com

Yenn: To the contributors of this book for sharing their stories and to Sunflower the cat for providing encouragement and purrs.

Wayne: I wish to thank each of the contributors for bringing *In Our Words* to life. My heartfelt love and thanks to my family, my mum Judy, dad Chris, brothers Rodney and Luke, and all my extended family. I love you.

My thanks and love to all my beautiful friends and those "sisters" of mine too. I am forever indebted to you all for your unwavering friendship, love, and support. It means so much to me.

To my nieces and nephews Violet, Sasha, Charlotte, Luca, and Max. I dedicate this book to each of you. Uncle Wayne loves you.

"**In Our Words** is a book I wish had been available when I was a teenager, grappling with issues of sexuality and disability. Like many of the contributors to this book, I experienced feelings of confusion and a lack of pride and confidence in myself and my place in the world.

Through story-telling and the sharing of experiences, at times searingly raw, this book draws on rich diversity and intersectionality to present a clear message: it is okay to be queer and disabled.

I commend Wayne and Yenn for putting together a wonderful compilation of queer and disabled life stories. This is a book that will be an invaluable addition to queer and disabled literature."

– **Dr Alastair McEwin** AM, Former Commissioner, Disability Royal Commission; Former Disability Discrimination Commissioner

Abstract

This book comprises personal reflections from a number of queer and disabled authors. Each chapter takes the form of a letter to the author's younger self, focusing on how they overcame barriers and discrimination to succeed in life.

The book is strongly based on ideas of the intersection of queer and disabled identity. People who are queer and disabled face a number of challenges around building a positive identity and coming to a place of self-acceptance and love. There is a lot of discrimination, stigma, ableism, homophobia, transphobia, and hatred for those who are queer and disabled. The journey to positive identity can be a long and difficult one. This book provides an example to others experiencing similar challenges and those who love and care for them. It is very personal and reflective and also promotes a sense of pride. The book focuses on responding to issues around discrimination, building a strong, proud identity, and using that identity to make change.

Keywords

Disability; Disabled; LGBTQIA+; Queer; Transgender; Gay; Lesbian; Inclusion; Journey; Social model of disability; Ableism

Contents

Foreword by Philippa Moss   xi

Introducing the editors: When Yenn met Wayne and Wayne met Yenn   xiv

Learning objectives   xx

Chapter 1   Introduction   1

Chapter 2   Wayne Herbert   13

Chapter 3   Dr Wesley Lim   27

Chapter 4   Kelly Vincent   35

Chapter 5   Zoe Simmons   45

Chapter 6   Dr Wenn Lawson   55

Chapter 7   Empress Eyrie   67

Chapter 8   Dr Emma Goodall   75

Chapter 9   Freya Pinney   81

Chapter 10   Ainslee Hooper   95

Chapter 11   Jack Brady   101

Chapter 12   Kat Reed   111

Chapter 13   Margherita Coppolino   117

Chapter 14   Yenn Purkis   133

Chapter 15   Summary   145

Suggested discussion topics   148

References   149

Recommended further reading   151

Index   153

Content warning

This book covers material which some may find triggering, including bullying, bigotry, mental illness, and suicide.

Foreword

This book explores identities – specifically the intersections of queer and disability identities. Identities are personal, but they are also how we present ourselves, so they are often very circumstantial, too. For example, I'm a queer woman, a mother, a partner. This is how I present myself in my role as the CEO of Canberra's leading LGBTQIA+ peer-led organization (Meridian), as a writer in my own right, and as a social entrepreneur.

I am brave. The courage of bravery has led me on the journey of a lifetime where I have met so many people with disability on the intersection of queerness. Both of the terms "disability" and "queer" mean different things to different people. Today, the word "queer" is a way for us to create space for those who have been othered by the LGBTQIA+ rights movement, by social norms and customs, and by outdated notions of gender. It is hardly surprising that those who have had to look at the world, and navigate it from the unique perspectives which their disability gives, are also providing inspiring perspectives on gender and sexuality for us all to benefit from.

I like to dream big and surround myself with brilliant people – it's a strategy I employ. Every day I see people doing great things in the world. What do they have in common? The courage to go after their dreams and make a positive impact. Wayne Herbert and Yenn Purkis's book, *In Our Words*, provides a message we all need to understand and we should all support in moving through life. It's a message of acceptance, courage, love, and kindness – that is what we need to overcome discrimination, ableism, homophobia, and transphobia.

In Our Words puts disability front and centre in its intersections with queer identity. This is so important in a world that undervalues these stories and sees them as niche rather than universal. Including 11 heartfelt letters to their younger selves, *In Our Words* passes on the wisdom they wish they'd had at the time. In this way, they provide hope to readers old and young that things can and will get better. These stories have the potential to offer us all a different perspective – the voice of the adult that your child self needed but wasn't there at the time. In this way, they can be a great tool in the healing process. Looking back at times in your life that have been difficult can help uncover different perspectives and bring forward the strength, courage, and resilience that drove you and can drive you once more.

Through the sharing of the stories and experiences of those on the intersection of disability and queer, *In Our Words* provides a sense of community and hope. These messages can only have the power they do because they are written by and from the experience of peers. Telling your own stories and learning from others who have fought hard to thrive and flourish is the key to supporting and affirming peers. The advice and information provided by the writers will be invaluable to people who are developing their identity at any life stage, and to anyone who wants to support and understand them. I hope that through this book – and every time one of us shares our story – there's another crack helping to break down discrimination, ableism, homophobia, and transphobia. It's time to be brave and bring this narrative into the spotlight.

Herbert and Purkis bring together a collection of stories which are all inspiring in their own right but, together, they make for an impressive, insightful, and stimulating read.

I commend *In Our Words* to you.

Philippa Moss

Introducing the editors

When Yenn met Wayne and Wayne met Yenn

I was part of the Disability Employment Australia national conference in 2016, being one of the speakers for the flagship conference event, which was a great debate on disability employment. The other people in the debate were influential folks in the world of disability and work and then there was me! I was really looking forward to this event as it was on a topic I am passionate about and was quite a prestigious speaking event.

The night before the conference I got the flu. I was really sick and only got two hours' sleep, but I am a bit of a workaholic and didn't want to let the conference organizers down! So, I got out of bed and caught the first flight of the day to Melbourne to attend the conference. I felt like absolute death. Apparently – according to conference delegates – my contributions to the great debate were fantastic. I didn't know this as I was primarily concerned with not falling off the stage or vomiting on the front row – both of which seemed quite likely as I took to the podium!

After my talk I was absolutely wrecked. I just wanted to go home and sleep. However, I started talking to a young person who was snappily dressed. Despite feeling monumentally crappy, I introduced myself. I was probably not at my most professional at this point, due to the flu and the lack of sleep and so forth. Anyway, this was what I said to this young man I had never met before…

"Hi. I'm Yenn. Do you know I have been thinking about Lady Gaga all day! You know that song 'Let's have some fun, this beat is sick, I want to take a ride on your disco stick'?" The young person – who turned out to be the person I now know as the awesome Wayne Herbert – said "I love Lady Gaga!" and so of course we had to be friends. We caught a flight home to Canberra together – well, I assume we did. I honestly don't remember much of the rest of that afternoon!

***

I love Lady Gaga. What actually is a disco stick? Hi Yenn, I'm Wayne. What Yenn didn't know is that I knew who they were. I was familiar with Yenn's work. I had admired their advocacy for some time. I had even read some of their previous books. I was aware of some of the circumstances that Yenn had experienced and how they had shaped the person they are. I was excited to finally meet in person and over our work and our willingness to advocate for positive change for people in our communities. I was aware that they had already published several books exploring various issues including autism. It was a chance meeting and a mutual respect for each other's work and a shared love of writing would give me a great idea. An idea that would set a course for a friendship and well, as they say, the rest is history.

***

A while later, Wayne asked me to launch his first book *Anecdotes of a Disabled Gay*, which I did. The launch was amazing – something I felt honoured to be a part of and a highlight of the year for the disabled and queer community in Canberra. The book was one of the best I have read on the topic. Wayne went on to do some really wonderful things including a TEDx talk, presentations all over the world and this book, to name a few. I have been at dozens of events where Wayne was the keynote speaker or MC and I have enjoyed all of them. And more recently Wayne asked me if I wanted to write a book with him – which became this book. It has been a very fruitful friendship – and we still both love Lady Gaga!

How this book came about

A while back Wayne got in touch with me (Yenn) and asked if I would like to write a book with him. "Yes!" was the emphatic response. We had a meeting at a cafe in Gungahlin, Canberra, where I live. Wayne wanted to write about being queer and disabled and overcoming challenges – a topic I am also passionate about, so I was keen too. We wanted to write about the intersection of queer identity and disabled identity. The idea was to write a letter to our younger selves telling them how they have overcome challenges, what success looks like for each person, and how despite the many and varied challenges they have become awesome people.

We thought it would be great to have contributions from other queer and disabled people, also writing to their teenage selves. I had a few people in mind to approach and Wayne had some too. We set about asking people to contribute and got a very positive response. Some people weren't able to do it but most of the people we approached were very keen and said yes. We ended up with 11 contributors.

The chapters came in and they were all amazing, covering different topics but also sharing many commonalities. For some people it was the first contribution to a book that they had written, while for others it was the last in a long line of publications. There are a range of common themes throughout including coming out, experiencing ableism, homophobia, transphobia and other bigotry, the impact of positive relationships, and coming to know and embrace disabled and queer identities. Many of the contributors are neurodivergent, some are gender divergent, and there are some with diverse sexuality. The contributors often have additional intersectional differences and experiences and belong to a range of other identity groups – such as First Nations, culturally and linguistically diverse people, and those who have had criminal justice system involvement and/or are of low socio-economic status.

***

I (Wayne) had a simple idea. To write a book that explored what success looks like for people who identified as a member of the queer and disabled communities. The opportunity to give many other members of our communities the chance to share their stories is something I am proud of. As this was my second book I wanted to continue to explore intersectionality and the lack of representation in literature and set about changing that. I think *In Our Words* will do just that. My hope is that this book reframes the conversation of disability and queer culture to one that fully recognizes the strength of our rich diversity and intersectionality as queer disabled people. I hope it challenges readers' perceptions, lifts the weight of low expectation, and inspires us to think about success in the face of the many and various forms of discrimination that continue to be experienced by queer and disabled people in our community. I am excited for *In Our Words* to take its rightful place in the conversation of disability and queer culture to create positive change. But beyond that I hope it finds a place in the hearts and minds of each of you, our readers.

I also wanted to work with someone else to reach out across our communities. It got me thinking about who I could work with on this project. I know, Yenn! That's when I reached out to Yenn to get their advice. I was thrilled they loved the idea and I was excited when they agreed to co-author the book with me. One of the key differences was that I wanted the book to be focused on success and what that looked like for each contributor. How, in the face of continued discrimination, the challenges of entrenched negative stereotypes, and the ever-present weight of low expectation, many different forms of success were indeed possible.

***

I (Yenn) am delighted to be a part of this book. Each chapter filled me with joy and enthusiasm when it arrived. I think it is empowering and positive and that it will make a big difference to both queer and disabled people and those working with us – or researching the topics of Disability studies and Queer studies. Writing a book with Wayne has been amazing. And coordinating the work of 11 contributors and empowering them to share their stories has also been very rewarding and enjoyable.

Wayne and I hope you will find this book really helpful. It went from an idea in a cafe to this final publication. We hope that you enjoy the stories and find the book helpful. There are thousands upon thousands of queer and disabled stories in the world. These are just a small sample. I have written 16 other books at the time of publication. This book is definitely one of my favourites of them all. I am so happy that Wayne wanted to write it with me.

Learning objectives

1. Exploring the identity and experiences of queer and disabled people.
2. Understanding the discrimination that is experienced by queer and disabled people.
3. Finding ways of advancing inclusive places for queer and disabled people.
4. Advancing understanding of the intersectionality of queer and disability.
5. Understanding how queer and disabled people can be empowered and have a sense of pride and positive identity.

1
Introduction

Welcome to this book! It is all about disability and queer identity. The book has a number of stories from queer and disabled authors. These take the form of each author writing a letter to their teenage self outlining how they overcame barriers to get to where they are now. The authors are Jack Brady, Kelly Vincent, Margherita Coppolino, Wenn Lawson, Emma Goodall, Empress Eyrie, Freya Pinney, Zoe Simmons, Wesley Lim, Ainslee Hooper, and Kat Reed. Wayne Herbert and Yenn Purkis contributed their stories too. The book also includes an overview of disabled and queer identities, coming out, representation, and allies.

Some words about words

The words we use demonstrate our understanding of a person, a group – or ourselves. Words are important and knowing the appropriate language is particularly important in the queer and disability space.

- **Queer** – An umbrella term meaning anyone who identifies as part of the "LGBTQIA+" acronym. Some people – especially older people – do not like the term queer as it was used as an insult by bigots in the past. Queer is a word which has largely been reclaimed, so for many people it is an inclusive term. It is important to be aware of the many interpretations of the word and not use it with people who find it offensive.

- **Transgender** – A person who identifies as a different gender to that which they were assigned at birth. Transgender is often shortened to trans. There are some terms for transgender people which are not appropriate and feed into bigotry and hate. Things like "cross dresser" or "trannie" are not OK.

- **Cisgender** – "Cis" is a Latin word meaning "on the same side as". Cisgender people are simply not transgender. Some cisgender people think it is an insult or slur but it is not. It is simply a way of saying a person is not transgender.

- **AFAB** – assigned female at birth

- **AMAB** – assigned male at birth

- **Pronouns** – Pronouns are the way we describe people in terms of their gender. There are many different pronouns people use, including he/him, they/them, she/her, they/she, xe/xeir, and he/they to name a few. Some people do not use pronouns at all! It is important to get people's pronouns correct. If you make a mistake, just apologize and resolve not to do it again. While pronouns are often part of identity for trans and gender-divergent people, they are not just about gender.

- **Intersex** – Intersex people have sex or reproductive body parts which are not truly masculine or feminine. Intersex variations are relatively common. Intersex people may identify as any gender or agender. It is not appropriate to call an intersex person "a hermaphrodite". Intersex people often have surgery when they are children to make their sex characteristics more typically male or female and this is done without their consent. This is not OK and is essentially violence and abuse.

- **Gender divergent** – Being gender divergent means your gender identity is not cisgender. Gender-divergent identities include non-binary, transgender, agender, two spirit, and many others.
- **Disability** – A disability is any condition of the body or mind that makes it challenging for the person with the condition to do certain activities and interact with the world around them. There are issues around the concept of what constitutes a disability, which will be outlined later in this book.
- **Neurodivergent** – Neurodivergent people are those who have neurology/brain wiring that is different to the "norm". Neurodivergent conditions include autism, ADD, ADHD, dyslexia, dyspraxia, Tourette's, and others.
- **Neurotypical** – Neurotypical simply means that a person isn't neurodivergent. Like the term cisgender, it is not an insult or criticism.

Disability and identity

Disability can be a fraught concept. When people think of disability they often think of deficits and negatives – that is, people lacking something and being unable to complete daily activities. Disability is seen as a predominantly negative thing. Many people pity disabled folk and even pray over them – whether they want this or not! Everyone has the right to identify in whatever way they choose. It is not appropriate to tell somebody else how they should identify. This book predominantly uses identity-first language (e.g., "disabled person" as opposed to "person with disability"). This reflects the social model of disability.

Social and medical models of disability

There are different models of disability including the medical model and the social model (People With Disability Australia, 2023). The medical model centres on the idea that someone has a medical condition which limits them. The problem is seen as being the disability, not society. However, the social model focuses on how disability is socially constructed. Disability in the social model is more the result of society not accepting or accommodating disabled people than them being broken or deficient. The social model can give rise to activism and inclusion. This book comes from the perspective of the social model of disability.

You can imagine the social model like this: picture a world where almost everyone is a wheelchair user. The world would be set up for people who are sitting down. This would mean non-wheelchair users would be disadvantaged – doorways would be too low and they would constantly need to be bending down. In this world not using a wheelchair would probably be seen as a disability – cue unwanted prayers and "inspiration porn" for those poor disadvantaged standing-up people! Or imagine a world where almost everyone was autistic. They would function very differently and neurotypical people would struggle to be understood and would probably face a load of stigma and bigotry – just like autistic people do in the world we live in now, where there are more neurotypical people than neurodivergent. In the social model, the main issue around disability is societal attitudes and barriers, not the health condition itself.

Disability discrimination

Disabled people face discrimination and exclusion. Advocacy and activism attempt to counter this. Disabled folk often need a strong sense of their own identity in order to navigate life. Our sense of identity can make a big difference. Disabled identities are growing and evolving and this is a good thing. Society needs to change to support, respect, and include disabled folks.

The workplace is often an environment where disabled people face discrimination. Some examples of this include:

- Not considering a job applicant who uses a mobility scooter;
- Dismissing an employee after finding out that she claimed workers' compensation in her last role;
- Not allowing a staff member to bring their assistance dog to work; and
- Excluding a disabled person from social activities at work.

(Disability Discrimination Victorian Equal Opportunity and Human Rights Commission, 2023)

Inspiration porn, micro-aggressions, and other issues

Disabled people, unfortunately, are often treated with what is known as "inspiration porn". This is a term coined by the late disability activist Stella Young. It refers to disabled people being seen as "inspirational" for doing everyday things. Author Yenn once had someone tell them that they were "inspirational" for taking the bus to work! The idea of disabled people being somehow inspirational is extremely fraught and a great many disabled people find it extremely infuriating and invalidating.

Inspiration porn is part of a number of attitudes around disability that are unhelpful. These include assumptions and stereotypes that are widely held. Author Yenn had someone at a conference they were speaking at ask if they "live at home with [their] mummy". (Yenn responded that they were in fact living with their cat in a property they were paying off with the salary from their highly paid professional job!) These attitudes are harmful but very common. There is also a myth that all disabled people are asexual or cannot engage in sexual intercourse. This is, of course, complete nonsense. Many disabled people have very healthy sexual appetites! And some are asexual, which is OK too.

Another issue relates to microaggressions. These are things like offhand comments that are offensive – intentionally or otherwise. They are common for people from any intersectional groups, including disability people and queer people. Misgendering trans people can be seen as a microaggression, as can telling an autistic person that they could "pass for normal". Telling people how they should identify is another form of microaggression. (For example, when someone criticizes a disabled person for using identity-first language – such as "I am Deaf".) Most of the time people do not realize that they are doing a microaggression but this does not make it any less invalidating and unpleasant for the person on the receiving end.

LGBTQIA+ identity

People who identify as lesbian, gay, bisexual, transgender, intersex, queer/questioning, and/or asexual are captured within the acronym LGBTQIA+. Historically, and in the present time, LGBTQIA+ people have been discriminated against and have faced bigotry and hatred, to the point of violence and murder on many occasions. In many countries, even now, being LGBTQIA+ can result in legal penalties such as imprisonment. Many LGBTQIA+ people do not disclose their identities for fear of being attacked and discriminated against.

Being proud as someone who identifies as LGBTQIA+ is a way of countering the hatred we so often face. Pride is a very important thing in LGBTQIA+ communities and enables people to like and value themselves and also address the hatred and bigotry. Pride can be seen as a political act and is a form of empowerment in a world which often does not empower queer folks.

Intersection of LGBTQIA+ and disabled identity

Many disabled people are also queer/LGBTQIA+. Some people think a person only has one sort of identity. So if you are queer then that is your only identity and if you are disabled then that must be your only identity. In fact, most people who belong to an "equity"-type group actually belong to more than one. Author Yenn is many kinds of queer, many kinds of disabled and has a history of poverty and criminal justice system involvement. They have a number of different identities and you may well have heard the word that describes this – intersectionality. Civil Rights activist Professor Kimberley Crenshaw came up with the concept of neurodiversity a while back. When the term was first used it referred mainly to the intersection of race and gender, but it is now used as a model that works for all "equity"-type groups.

Intersectional disadvantage means that each element of diversity you have compounds the disadvantage faced. So, a queer, First Nations, disabled person has the disadvantage they face pretty much multiplied by three. It is not really as simplistic as that but the principle of multiplying disadvantage remains. Many of the authors of this book experience intersectional disadvantage on many levels.

Because of this, the sense of identity and positive self-knowledge and pride that we have as queer and disabled people is extremely important. Events like Pride Month, International Day for People with Disability, and the Sydney Gay and Lesbian Mardi Gras are a great way of demonstrating pride and empowering us. However, as disabled people we can be excluded from some queer spaces and as queer people we can be excluded from some disabled spaces. Building a sense of pride and addressing bigotry and exclusion wherever we find it is essential.

Coming out

Coming out – particularly in the LGBTQIA+ space – can be extremely challenging. There are lots of spheres in which to come out. The situation that I imagine most people think of is a gay or trans young person coming out to their family, but there are many elements of coming out. Author Yenn came out as non-binary first on Facebook! Being out or being closeted are considerations pretty much all queer folks have to decide on. And for disabled people, sometimes the only place they are not out is at work. But disclosing an invisible disability in the workplace can be very fraught and people can worry about how their disability will be received by their managers and colleagues.

One thing about coming out is that it may need to happen multiple times. It isn't as if you come out to your family and then that is the only time you need to. Coming out is often an ongoing process. It can be highly anxiety provoking to come out. A good approach is to decide who you are going to tell, when you will do it, and what you will say. It can help to pick the "low hanging fruit" – in other words, the first few times you do it come out to someone – or people – who you are confident will not be bigoted. This can help to give you confidence to come out to people you are less sure will respond well.

Of course, there is no law saying that you need to come out but it often makes life easier and empowers you to be your authentic self. One person coming out at work can support and encourage others to also come out.

Representation

Representation in this context refers to where disability and queer people are found in the world – examples include politics, popular culture, music, or sports. While things have improved lately, there are still a lot of challenges in this space. Representation is really important. What we see determines how we think about a group in society. If you watch *The Big Bang Theory*, you are going to have a different view of autism than if you watch a documentary featuring autistic adults. Some media representation can support respect and inclusion while some echoes stereotypes and unhelpful assumptions.

If you watch the 1980s British sitcom *Are You Being Served?*, which has a very stereotypical gay male character, you will get a different picture of gay male experience than if you watch an empowering film about queer experience such as *Paris is Burning* or *Milk*. Some representations drive and reiterate unhelpful assumptions and stereotypes while others can empower and challenge. And the messages we get from these representations impact on how we will view and treat people from inclusion groups.

It is essential to have respectful and inclusive representation in order for people to have a better understanding of diversity and inclusion. This is particularly true for people who do not belong to any diverse groups and who get all or most of their knowledge from popular culture and it influences how they interact with people.

Representation has improved in recent years but there is still a way to go until we reach a truly inclusive society. For it to be effective, we need people with a personal lived experience to be in positions of representation. For example, if you have a transgender character in a movie, then get a transgender person to play the role. We need disabled and queer people in every role in society – in healthcare, education, advocacy, entertainment, industry, politics and government administration, agriculture... everywhere. There is a saying that "if you can't see it, you can't be it". This is a very important concept in this area.

Allies

An ally is a person who does not themselves belong to an equity group but who supports and stands up for those who do. For example, author Yenn is not intersex themselves but they identify as an ally to intersex people and they have signed the Darlington Statement for Intersex rights. The Darlington Statement is a joint consensus statement or charter made by Australian and Aotearoa/New Zealand intersex organizations and independent advocates, in March 2017. It sets out the priorities and calls by the intersex human rights movement, under six headings: a preamble; human rights and legal reform; health and wellbeing; peer support; allies; and education, awareness, and employment (Darlington Statement, 2017).

Allies can make a huge difference. One really handy attribute of an ally is that people who are bigoted are more likely to listen to an ally than the person they are bigoted against (The University of Melbourne, 2023). There is a story which was doing the rounds of the Internet a few years back. An African American woman was being harassed by a racist shop assistant. The African American woman's sister-in-law – who was pale-skinned – called the shop assistant out on her behaviour. This made a much bigger impact than if the woman on the receiving end of the bigotry had called it out. Allies can make a big difference.

About privilege

Most people have some areas of privilege. For example, author Yenn is white and middle class. Rather than feeling guilt about having these areas of privilege, it is far better to use that privilege to support and advocate for others who face disadvantage in the areas where you experience privilege.

2
Wayne Herbert

Wayne Herbert is an International Speaker, Presenter, MC, Author, Comedian, Disability, and LGBTQIA+ community activist.

Wayne walks the talk. He has worked with a range of Australian and international government agencies and organizations as well as previously serving as a member of the ACT Government Disability Reference Group, and as deputy chairperson of the ACT Government's LGBTQIA+ Ministerial Advisory Council. He is also a highly experienced Not for Profit board director and is a member of the Australian Institute of Company Directors.

Wayne is the author of the hugely successful book, *Anecdotes of a Disabled Gay* and his 2017 TEDx Canberra feature has had thousands of views.

Intelligent, unique, funny, and thought-provoking, Wayne Herbert challenges insights into the issues faced by the LQBTQIA+ community and people with disabilities.

Welcome to my world
Wayne's story

It was a late October afternoon. This moment has been several months in the making. On the other hand, was it a lifetime? There you are standing on stage left. In almost complete darkness, alone, your heart beating fast in anticipation. The almost capacity audience is waiting to see something. To see what? You look into the distance and the space seems almost endless. You then see a burning bright white light suddenly illuminate a single red circle that is centre stage. You can see heat in the air and what looks like flickers of dust or glitter.

They are waiting for you. You look down at your feet for just a few seconds, but it feels much longer. You are shaking just a little and feel unsteady… hey! What is new? Nevertheless, you know you've got this. Yes, you do.

What will they see? Me? What will they think?

They are waiting for you. The full you. The complete you. Just as you are.

You step out. The red circle is just there. You will see. They will see.

It's showtime.

Hello. It's me. Yes, Wayne, that is you. Standing there. I guess some might say life is a performance. A full collection of moments. All pivotal moments in shaping you, even this one. So many people you are yet to meet are pivotal too – they inspire and support you. Your colleagues, mostly fearless women. You look up to them. They help guide and craft your career, your LGBTQIA+ community, your family. You know them, of course; your lovers, your friends old and new, Josh and Shaun, and those "sisters" of yours too.

You were always an activist. You really admire the late, great Stella Young. You admire her work. Stella once said, "the magnitude of discrimination and stigma faced by people with disability in

Australia cannot be underestimated". This must change. You, Wayne, are an important part of this much-needed change. By no means do you do this alone, but you just wait and see. On the other hand, read on and let me tell you just how you do it.

Oh, and right now just as I sit down to start to write, Mariah Carey is playing in the background. Her words, her music, resonate with you in many ways. "They do try hard to make me feel/ That I don't matter at all/ But I refuse to falter in doing what I believe/ Or lose faith in my dreams/ 'Cause there's a light in me/ That shines brightly/ Yes, they can try/ But they can't take that away from me/ From me" (Carey and Warren, 1999).

They say time flies when you are having fun, though life is not always fun, but what I want you to know is that it will not always be this way. Things change for the better through struggle and strife, and from what seems like endless pain and fear comes success and triumph. Honestly, you just do not know it yet. Your family does. Mum and Dad often tell you how strong you are, and you often look to them when you are struggling. They are always right there with you in every success and the many failures, do not worry.

You now work to ensure awareness and support for everyone on the intersections, just like you. You still want to let people in to be part of the change conversation, wherever that is. You want them to get to know you, really know you. You have a unique way of doing this that will see you take spaces not often occupied by disabled people. Let me tell you that a seat at the table should never be the apex of privilege for you and other leaders with disability. It is simply an expectation. Yet, despite all your accomplishments, it means so much to you, but it would mean even more to share it with someone. I guess in a way I am sharing it with you, yes you, the reader. I never want to be described as vulnerable and weak, and never wanted to be marginalized. You soon discover you are forced to be marginalized by social and political design and in some ways political choices often made by mostly non-disabled people. You wonder whether they would lead differently if in time they became a person with disability. In a more inclusive way, like you? Will we grow in our shared understanding of each other? Because after all, we may all be people with disability at some point in our lives.

Wayne, you are so young. Everyone called you Pooh. Guess what? They still do now. It is true you may be a little awkward at times, unsure, lost, and fearful. You may not always "fit in" and you may not be "popular". But you don't mind that. You just want to be free to be you. This seems easy, right? It is not. If you ask me if the struggle is worth it – yes, it is! I know this now; you may, and then again may not, be surprised by where you have ended up because you are right where you belong. You are a leader with a vision and a story, a wit, and a warmth only you can share, and you do just that.

The path to get here may not have been as easy as you imagined, and in some ways you have had to work twice as hard to get half the recognition … but all I can say is look at you now. Many people look up to you and look to you for advice. Just look at everyone looking at you now.

You made it through all the difficult, trying times. Even when you thought so many times you would not. You continue today in all parts of your career to give voice and visibility to those like you who are often overlooked and excluded and demand to see and ensure genuine inclusion.

To understand how you got here, we need to start at the very beginning; someone famous said that is a very good place to start.

I remember it as if it were yesterday: I think it was Year Four News. The topic was: "Something important to you" or "what is something you are proud of?"

I recall others in my class talking about their skills at ball sports (something I lack unfortunately, but you improve, don't worry), their family, friends, and beloved family pets. Some even had props. I had my 'My First Pony' in my bag, a gift from my grandparents. My brothers and I loved them. On this day, I did not talk about my pony. I simply stood up and said, "I am Wayne; I have cerebral palsy".

A classmate even called out: "Is that a transformer?" with a level of enthusiasm I had never seen before.

Well, unfortunately, as talented and skilled as you are Wayne, you have no superhuman powers. Mum and Dad just say you've got a big mouth. Just Wayne. Completely as you are. In this moment included in a classroom with my peers. Not in a separate classroom and not behind bars or separated by a fence, a wall, or a locked door (for some disabled people this still happens). You will continue to wonder why we teach young people that treating disabled people like this within our education system is somehow right or just. It is not. Why do we do it? But there you are, standing right there. You never attended a segregated school. Nor did Mum and Dad, your family, or your close friends ever accept that you wouldn't be included. In many ways you helped them understand you, you allowed people in. You always smiled and laughed even if it was through tears and pain. You will often wonder why. Thankfully, Mum and Dad had an unwavering commitment to ensuring that I was afforded equity and equality. What a different path my life may have taken without their support and fearless and fair advocacy. What this meant was that I had always known my disability or sexuality did not define me. They are aspects of who Wayne the activist is, and you should be very proud of that.

It was this experience at around eight or nine years of age that would shape my belief that genuine inclusion changes lives. It did mine. You have shown what is possible and continue to make sure your voice and the voices of other people just like you are heard, valued, and respected. Yet the privileged and powerful will want you to believe that you are weak, marginalized, and vulnerable. But you never really subscribed to that view. On the other hand, I prefer to think that it is the powerful and privileged who are chronically obsessed with keeping you and people like you marginalized and vulnerable. Good luck to them; the tide is shifting. Advocates long before you have set a course for change, for choice, for control.

As I write this, I am sitting in your house. On the wall hangs a painting of you. I love it. The painting is not just of one of you, but two images of you, or as I like to call it, the versions of me. One was never enough. Although I want you to know this, you are enough. You always have been. I am sorry, though, for all the time you spent worrying about what other people think of you. When I look at you now, in one image, to be honest I see that deep pain and I am reminded of the hurt, the homophobia, the violence, the ridicule, and the exclusion you have faced and in so many ways you have overcome. I look at it every morning and I am reminded of the pain that in some way never leaves you, and for that I am sorry.

The good thing is that it fuels you and energizes you always. You are driven and determined. That is why in the other image I see grit and determination, a focus that will see you through. You may not see it now, but I do, trust me. But how things have changed.

You have long believed that you have strengths, talents, and skills and are powerful and influential. You have always wanted to have a lasting positive impact on everyone you meet, and you surely do. However, as people with disability, we live and work in environments, systems, and structures that make us vulnerable. You grow tired of hearing that and set about reframing the conversation in a way only you know how. Let's look at the things you did, Wayne. You were a failed beauty queen, a failed reality TV contestant; you would even audition for many theatre productions and fail at that too and then be asked to do the lighting. This was even after taking your own props, including designer puppies, in a handbag to try at least to further persuade the directors to cast you, only to once again, you guessed it, fail then too. If that is not resilience, I do not know what is. However, Wayne, do not worry, you do indeed find your stage eventually. A red circle that is the TEDx stage, which started it all. Despite this success you still fail to get into pubs, because they think you are intoxicated. It is not that at all – you are intoxicating. Funny story, you were almost arrested not so long ago. For what, do you ask? For daring to walk into a pub. You did not even have a single drink, then suddenly several policemen surrounded you, and you thought to yourself, "What? It really is true; 'my milkshake does bring all the boys to the yard' ".

When I think of the journey to being the strong, confident Wayne that you are, do you remember the question my mum and dad asked so many times… don't get scared. It was just "are you happy?" Simple, right? It is all that matters to Mum and Dad. I remember too how you wanted a coming-out story. You know you never had to. At the time you wondered to yourself if it was that obvious. To be honest with you, yes. The entire family wouldn't want it any other way. Yes, you wanted a coming-out party. You planned it in your head. The vision of me parading down the stairs to Kylie's "Shocked". Trust me, my family were not shocked, they knew long before I did. How? What gave it away? As a teenager you didn't appreciate that fully, but you do now. Mum and Dad always said it was just and always will be who you are. Here I was thinking it was my obsession with the Spice Girls, my love of Kylie, or my fascination with Madonna and all the time it was just me. In fact, when you talk with Mum and Dad about it, they simply say "we know; we have always known. We love you." Three simple words that would be transformative. That was it. No party. No parade. Just love, acceptance, and support.

However, you should know Mum and Dad did worry about how you would cope with others, with the world around you. They always worry. You do all you can to reassure them. But they are right to worry sometimes. The reality of homophobia and disability discrimination are too much to bear. You often wonder if it is right to be angry or upset. When all you hope for is genuine happiness, and that will often seem out of reach, ever elusive, is it just a dream to live a life free of this fear? Let me tell you it is. Although that fear and anxiety still comes in waves, it ebbs and flows. In moments you can be reminded of just how far you have come. If you could only see how you have grown to understand yourself, as you are, with all your fears, failures, and fabulousness. It turns out you will be more than fine.

I know even being so sure of who you are, Wayne, came at a cost, as you were so young. I know sometimes you feel powerless, I know you are sometimes scared, I know you sometimes feel as if it is all too much, and you just want the pain to end. And in the darkest of times you think "should I just end this?" All I can say is that I am so glad you held on, because things are getting better. With your courage, change is possible, although it can seem to take an eternity. Oh, you haven't found that "someone" although there are reality shows for that now, so maybe you could audition. You are yet to get married; in fact you are happily single. Oh, do you remember when you discovered that in parts of Australia at the time it was illegal to be gay? That was difficult and confronting to process as a young person. We finally have marriage equality, and you were in the gallery of Parliament when this finally passed. I guess this is a good time to talk with you about relationships. After all, your self-confidence will only take you so far.

You often wonder about gay culture and where you will find your place, and about how others view you, your body, your views, and opinions. Are you too loud? Too outspoken? Is that why you have sometimes found these situations trying? Despite this you engage actively, proudly, and fiercely in your community, only to see your friends crave connection too. You are not alone in this. In fact, are we all lonely? Are we all swiping right? Is Mr Right

Now just a few metres away? Is my body offensive? Should I be ashamed? Am I unlovable? Unfuckable? No way. Hell no! Forget that, look at you! However, you do think deeply about the ideal image that you and others are seeking. And why do you think others look past you? It could be them, Wayne, and maybe it could be you sometimes too. Let that fear go.

We are still fighting, though, for other members of our rainbow community, a fight you are proud to be a part of. Of course, you want to get married (maybe) and one day, maybe, be a success like Muriel Heslop. You still remember going to watch that with Mum in Ballina on the annual family Christmas holiday. You still watch it today and recite your favourite lines. "Since I've met you… I haven't listened to one ABBA song. That's because now my life is as good as an ABBA song. It's as good as 'Dancing Queen'"; or then again maybe"… I'll go on this holiday and I'll sleep with a thousand men" (*Muriel's Wedding*, 1994), and you, Wayne, are to this day a dancing queen. Just ask the guests in the hotel across the street and you are yet to go on that holiday. Don't worry, there is still time.

You have been loved and in love and been successful and unsuccessful in love. Some of your Grindr and Tinder dates have been more fleeting moments, interludes; you now describe yourself as chronically single. Somewhat by choice.

It seems far easier to find multiple Mr Right Nows rather than Mr Right. However, as the saying goes, all good things come to those who wait, right? Well, I am still waiting.

Oh, I almost forgot, Mum called today. She cannot wait for you to visit. Dad cannot wait for us all to share a drink and reminisce. You will be there with all the family. It is important that you do.

It has been quite some time between visits, and you are all only getting older. You have always understood each other so well, you always have. You do now, in even more ways. How life works in mysterious ways. You will see.

You, yes you, will set about changing the conversation around disability, diversity, inclusion, and intersectionality. You have a strong sense of social justice and have found your voice and you work hard to support others to do the same. I can tell you it all started one fateful morning when you were sitting on the edge of the bath talking to Mum as she brushed her teeth. Mum always had a way of cutting through and getting to the heart of the matter… Then came that question… you still laugh about it now, but at the time you just did not quite know how much it would mean. You do now. That question would prove beyond doubt that Mum is always aware. Mum is busily brushing her teeth and through the ever-expanding toothpaste foam she says, "So Wayne, do you have a girlfriend?"

"No!" I reply.

"Well do you have a boyfriend?"

"No!"

"Somebody you love." And then without hesitation, "Well, for God's sake, are you at least masturbating yet?"

Despite this unwavering support that continues today, you will at times find the world difficult to navigate. You will spend much time questioning yourself to the point of making yourself sick. Really sick for a time. You will feel filled with shame, because you see your identity (both your sexuality and disability) as two of your greatest strengths, but others not so much. They will see these as weaknesses and a reason to subject you to unthinkable acts of violence, homophobia, physical and emotional abuse, and trauma. Even now, there are some experiences that you cannot bring yourself to put into words.

You will have endless questions and sometimes find very few answers about the ways people treat you, the violence you have been faced with, the homophobia, the discrimination, all for simply going out into the world and being you. You seem to always be asking yourself, "Why? How can this happen to me? Will this ever end? Will things get better? Can I be free to just be me or shall I just give up? End it." These thoughts will linger. They scare you. I know it seems relentless, but I promise you it will change. It will change for the better. Just not now. The pain sometimes feels relentless.

In private, in the most testing times, you cannot find words to describe how you feel. You struggle to breathe and in the darkness of night you hope for better. There are times, many times, when you lie awake anxious, breathless, and it hurts. You are so young and often lie awake at night thinking "Will tomorrow bring much of the same? Will I be OK?" All I can say is hold on.

You were, and in some ways still are, the regular subject of cruel jokes, violence, bullying, and harassment. Simply being confident to be exactly who you are, as Mum and Dad told me to do almost every day, was much, much harder said than done. You are the oldest of three children; you grew up in a small country town. You still sometimes feel it now; the memories come flooding back occasionally, even if just in fleeting moments. I know you felt very isolated and alone at times; you were often confused as you were surrounded by the loving caring messages of family and friends and confronted head-on with the harsh reality of homophobia, violence, and abuse outside the home. It was real. It was frightening. You would be forgiven for being upset, even angry, I am sure. Despite these experiences you are not. You smile, you laugh, you lead. You set about changing course.

You are a leader now. You always have been. Your inner activist sets about changing the conversation from one far too often saturated in limitation, almost as if all LGBTQIA+ people with disability are drowning in deficit. We rarely get to speak of our talents, skills, capacity, and potential. What if we are living a good life? But you find yourself regularly listening to "leaders" perpetuating that tired and misguided view far too often, one you strongly oppose, of course. Your work leads you to ensure that you encourage every disabled person to always refuse to settle for anything less than the opportunity to experience success, to be the best they can be, and to experience equity and equality. And you want the opportunity, too, for all people like you to see the images and hear the voices, stories, and experiences as told by us in our words.

Do you remember when I said earlier that Mum called? She calls often just to talk. Just to hear your voice sometimes. You should know that Mum has Parkinson's disease now; it has been something she has been dealing with for a few years. In some ways, you both understand each other even more because of this. Now, in these moments, you just want to be there for Mum just as she still is for you, and you are.

You have comfort in knowing that you have discovered a newfound connection with both Mum and Dad as together as a family we face these new and unknown daily challenges in ways that I am sure Mum feels you always did too. Mum is your pillar of strength, as is your dad. Just as they were all those years ago, they are today your biggest supporters. After all, they have both shaped the person you are. I hope you know you make them proud. So proud.

Like those who know and love you. Trust me, just as Pink plays in the background (you do not know who she is yet), everyone wants you to "stay unfiltered and loud, you'll be proud of that skin full of scars …" (Pink, 2021).

You know what, Wayne? I say fuck your fears! Though there have been many tears, you are fabulous. There is so much more to do, but hey, when it is all said and done, just thanks for being you. You know what, that is success right there. Look at you. Keep living proudly and showing people what is possible. Be open and let yourself be vulnerable on your terms. Who knows what is next? I do, just you wait and see. Step by step it turns out you will be more than just fine.

Oh, and lastly, by the way, this is your second book. And look at you travelling Australia and the world speaking. And you are about to board yet another plane and widely share your story of success with people all over the world. That is not bad, hey? Give the audience what it is they want; more anecdotes from a life lived proudly and loudly, from you, Wayne, the disabled gay.

The world is your stage Wayne, and it is all yours now. You are right where you belong.

Shine on.

3
Dr Wesley Lim

Dr Wesley Lim is a Lecturer in German Studies at the Australian National University. His research focuses on the intersection of literary studies, German studies, dance studies, and performance studies. In particular, he analyses representations of and discourses on dance and the moving body in Germanic literature and on the screen from the nineteenth through the twenty-first century. He has published in journals like *German Quarterly*, *German Studies Review*, and *Dance Research Journal*. His first book *Dancing with the Modernist City: Metropolitan Dance Texts around 1900* (forthcoming with the University of Michigan Press) deals with interpenetrating depictions of dance and city space in modernist texts. He is currently working on the first comprehensive study of East German figure skating culture and on a book project with Michelle Ho (National University of Singapore) on Asian masculinities in contemporary figure skating.

Recalibrating the senses towards disabled movement

I had arranged to meet him for Thai food in the evening. When I arrived at the meeting point, I recognized him from his picture. Carrying a leather bag over his shoulder, he wore a t-shirt, pants, and dress shoes without socks. After I greeted and hugged him, we went to look for a table, and then I noticed that he had an unusual walk. I did not make any remark. Then we ordered our dishes and had the best time, chatting about everything. This was the first time I met Wayne Herbert.

This paper performs a reading of Wayne as represented in a YouTube video of his TEDx talk "Anecdotes of a disabled gay" (Herbert, 2017), in which he first provides meta-commentary concerning people's first impressions upon seeing him in social situations. Secondly, he extrapolates the wider social and political implications of being a queer and disabled individual. Theoretically, my paper engages with concepts of **impression formation, stereotypes, and individuating information** and is, furthermore, informed by my personal academic expertise in (German) cultural studies, dance studies, and performance studies. In line with the **continuum model** (Fiske and Neuberg, 1990), which aims to build new categories through observed individual characteristics of others instead of stereotypes, I argue that Wayne's fashion and, particularly, his gait demand a recalibration of the senses and a disruption of current meaning-making associated with disabled movement. This article more broadly highlights the importance of movement and its meaning in everyday society.

Impression formation occurs with anyone that we meet for the first time in our everyday social setting – coffee shop employees, doctors, hairdressers, bouncers, airport security, etc. During this initial interaction, "we immediately begin to form an impression of them, their personality traits, motivations, and abilities". (McLaughlin, 2014, 429). On the one hand, because of social conditioning, **stereotypes** often shape our initial impression of an individual's personality and aura. These are based particularly on age, gender, ethnicity, and occupation. For the purposes of this paper, I would like to add bodily movement to this list. On the other hand, through our interaction with this individual, we can begin to discern **individuating information** based on observed behaviours (McLaughlin, 2014, 429). These visual examinations help us to recognize more personal or idiosyncratic actions which culminate in a more unique individuality. According to Fiske and Neuberg, a **continuum model** can arise in which we form initial impressions based on stereotypes but then, depending on our desire for more engagement, we may take hold more onto the individuating factors and form completely new categories (Fiske and Neuberg, 1990). And indeed, I think this last model continues throughout the life of the interaction between people and takes on varying amounts of stereotypes as well as individuating information to produce an eternally evolving perspective.

In addition to using these terms to analyse Wayne's TEDx talk, I would like to introduce some other methods from the realm of cultural studies, dance studies, and performance studies that will influence my reading. Often derived from literary studies, cultural studies dehierarchializes its view by looking beyond high art "literature". Indeed, almost any text or object – photographs, films, texts, newspapers, YouTube, live performance of any kind, etc. – can be a subject of study. Particularly useful in this analysis will be "close reading": this method intimately analyses a small sampling of texts, objects, or phenomena to emerge with a meaning which might not have been completely apparent in the beginning. In addition to this, dance studies often look at movement and efforts to identify semiotic meaning. And performance studies treat the relationship between "performer" and "spectator" as not just in a theatrical stage space but as a part of everyday life (e.g., protests, demonstrations, public speeches, childbirth, walking around in the park, grocery shopping). Richard Schechner has characterized performance studies as being "sympathetic to the avant-garde, the marginal, the off-beat, the minoritarian, the subversive, the twisted, the queer, people of color, and the formally colonized" (Schechner, 2013). Again, since nearly anything could be subject to close analysis, disability studies and queer studies importantly fit into this paradigm.

Wayne's TEDx talk entitled "Anecdotes of a disabled gay" appeared on 13 November 2017 and has to date received around 5.7k views. Emerging on the YouTube platform gives it a virtual performance space to be viewed countless times and allows any viewer to also make comments. Focusing on the narrative experiences of individuals, TED is "dedicated to researching and sharing knowledge that matters through short talks and presentations" (TED, 2019). At the start of the video, Wayne makes his way towards the red dot in the middle of the stage to signify the start of his performance. Tacitly he cues the audience to cease talking and to listen to him. He wears slim blue jeans and a white t-shirt. On this shirt, we see a blonde woman's face with only the letters "RIS" visible, as his dark maroon sports jacket obscures the rest. A white frame printed on the t-shirt surrounds the image of the woman and further obscures her face. Of course, this only piques the audience's interest to see if more about his curious t-shirt will be revealed. Wearing grey sneakers, Wayne has short brown hair with a slightly extended fringe that appears to be flat ironed. He is also equipped with a slim, translucent microphone.

Wayne's fashion choices demonstrate a hybridized look that encompasses continuous combinations of business with casual and individuated personality with stereotypes. The jeans read as casual, while the t-shirt – upon closer inspection – displays the name "TRISH", once he reveals all the letters. On looking closer, the woman also appears to be bearded, with her mouth seductively open. Even though I don't know who Trish is, the ethos of the masculine facial hair and the spectacular aesthetics remind me of a queer drag performer. Indeed, the design of the t-shirt begs one to keep looking and inspecting. The dark maroon blazer reminds one of a more formal, masculine sports-look but the non-heteronormative selection of the colour may mildly queer the aesthetic. His hair reflects a Japanese style, which alludes to his time in Japan and being influenced by Asian forms of masculinity. His muted grey shoes give a sportier or casual look. Indeed, based on a reading of his appearance, not just on stereotypes – whether he contemplated his outfit and the aesthetics that he was relaying – Wayne's style does map on to his intersectional identity. In fact, to be clear with the audience, he didactically lists his identities at the beginning of his talk: gay/queer man, occasional drag queen, a senior leader in the disability services sector, and disabled individual with cerebral palsy. And although he did not include this in his list – but it becomes evident in his jokes – he also dabbles in the stand-up comedic arts. While we may have ascertained many of these identity markers as stereotypical through his fashion choices, for those features that did not come through clearly he at least then gives his own individuating information through speech, instead of our necessarily needing to observe him. Thus, the negotiation of the continuum model begins as soon as we see Wayne enter the stage.

While I have just focused on his appearance in the previous section, I will now concentrate on the significance of his gait as a visual signifier. He walks in the small enclosure of the proverbial red TEDx talk dot, and then remarks that the spectator might have noticed his gait as he approached – as a way of forming their first impression of him. However, the video only catches two of his steps, which may not have been perceived by the viewer as being an unusual gait. Building on his explicit physical demonstration, Wayne highlights verbally that people's first impression of him is often based on the way that he moves: "Because of the way I walk, I give myself the coveted title of Australia's cheapest and most convincing drunk." Here arises both the humour that he observes in his own situation but also the seriousness of what first impressions and the signifying importance of movement do for one's reading of Wayne, particularly from an ableist view. Within an Australian context, and as a part of its historically adopted British drinking culture, the high occurrence of alcoholism and "performance" of an intoxicated state in social spaces influences how the hegemonic society perceives his gait as being drunk. This may have been different had he grown up in the US, Europe, or Asia. Due to Wayne's lack of balanced, smooth, and buoyant steps, hegemonic Australians classify him automatically as drunk and deny him entry into establishments. Unfortunately, the power of first impressions through visual and kinetic cues leads us first to stereotypical understandings which may or may not correspond to their individuating characteristics. This might be why societies often place a great deal of importance on appearance, even if it does not correspond to the existential condition of the individual. The stereotype vs individuation paradigm seems to map well onto the German terms **Schein** and **Sein**. Besides rhyming beautifully with or without the "ch", the former refers to the often "deceptive" appearance, which does not necessarily always correspond to the latter ("reality" in this context).

I believe Wayne's gait should demand a recalibration of the senses to view all kinds of non-normative movement in a social space with new meanings. In dance studies, the study of movement addresses the quality, style, and aesthetics of movement but also looks at the social and political context in which dance happens. While hegemonic beauty is often the predominant form of aesthetics, it also more generally means how an object or phenomenon affects our five senses. Indeed, it is important to break away from commercial beauty and to also embrace the numerous other ways that our bodies can feel and express themselves. Both Eastern and Western Modernist and contemporary art often aim at evoking different affect besides beauty. While everyone's gait is unique, Wayne's is visually striking and different than most. His asymmetrical rhythm causes him to bob from side to side and derives from the amount of mobility and range of motion of his legs. His feet and legs do not have the extension of normative ones. The individuating features of his walk – resulting from the formation of his body during birth, operations, and physio – give rise to his unique style of walking. Thus, his walk is informed by both natural proclivity as well as invasive procedures – both medical and societal.

Given the distinct features of a walk, some people can visually and aurally recognize someone just by the way they walk. While some people would not like to be revered as a piece of artwork, I know Wayne would not mind. However, this also runs the risk of idolizing and fetishizing the disabled body. As a result, I would argue for a middle ground, like the continuum model that aims for both the stereotypes and the individuating characteristics manifesting themselves into a unique body roaming about the earth. I hope that people become more aware of hegemony and open to different forms of movement: not necessarily in an artistic but in an accepting, humanist, and empathetic sense.

I like to think that I have also engaged in the continuum model during my interactions with Wayne since I've known him. We are certainly beyond the point of first impressions as now he is one of my closest "sisters".[1] I can both see and not see his walk now. My perception continually changes. I still learn new things about Wayne every day. For example, while we were at a holiday house on the South Coast, I was doing ballet barre work on the railing of the balcony outside. I demonstrated rolling-through-the-foot exercises that form the building blocks for **tendu** and **dégagé**. Wayne disclosed to me that he had metal implanted into his foot and leg to help him walk. He tried doing the exercise with me, and I reflected on his revelation.

4
Kelly Vincent

Kelly Vincent is a writer, director, poet, actor, and disability rights advocate. They are probably best known for their former role as a Member of the South Australian Parliament where their major achievements included the Disability Justice Plan, a nation-leading change to the way victims, offenders, and witnesses with disabilities are treated in the justice system.

As a policy nerd, Kelly loves working with organizations to help them become more accessible and inclusive, especially for disabled and LGBTQIA+ people. Their first book, *Dandelion Heart*, a collection of essays and poems on living with disabilities, was published by Debut Books in 2021. Kelly is Creative Director at True Ability, a disabled persons' theatre company where they are passionate about using the arts to help marginalized people find their voice and uncover skills they never knew they had.

Kelly is available as a freelance writer, workshop facilitator, policy adviser, and speaker. Their favourite thing about being autistic is probably using their later-in-life diagnosis to help people access the support and self-confidence that Kelly did not have pre-diagnosis. Kelly's favourite stimming activity at the time of writing is going through the carwash.

www.kellyvincent.com.au

Kelly's story – Dear younger Kelly…

Right. Letter to my younger self. Let me think about how to do this.

To begin this exercise, I got the two of us to sit down together. I asked you to write a list of words that describe you, saying that I would write a list of words that do not describe you.

I closed my eyes and I saw the two of us. Me nearly thirty-five years old, you maybe eight or nine, sitting on the floor together, my back resting against the footplates of my wheelchair. You not wanting to sit on the ground and opting instead to rest on the back of your walking frame, your impressive physical strength allowing you to do so despite your walking frame not actually having a seat. You asked me why I haven't spoken to you in so long. I told you that there are some things you are probably not old enough to hear yet. But suffice it to say that life has been a bit difficult for the last few years and that, while this might be hard for you to understand at the moment, I stopped contacting you for a while to keep us both safe. Then I told you why I brought us together today.

I handed you a piece of paper and a pen and said, "Kelly, I want you to write a list of words that you think describe you. And not just the easy ones; the first things that come to mind. The generic ones. Dig deep and find the words you really think about yourself".

"Okayyyy…" you said, clearly a bit annoyed that I had disappeared for so long without adequate explanation, only to return with homework. "What are you going to do?" you asked, nodding your head at the piece of paper I had in front of me.

I smiled.

"I am going to write a list of words that I think do **not** describe you."

We sat like that for five or ten minutes. Or, let's be honest, it could have been ten minutes, it could have been ten hours. We've always been a bit time blind when we are focusing on something deeply interesting to us, which is why Mum has more than once come into our bedroom to find us still reading, not aware that it has grown dark around us. And even once, unaware that a papercut had been staining the pages of a precious book sticky and red.

Eventually, with a big sigh, you look up from your page and say, barely above a whisper, "Finished."

I nod and we trade papers.

Reading through your list, my heart leaps into my throat (not literally). As you get older and study writing more, you'll get used to these things called "metaphors" and "similes". Even though I was expecting this, the harshness of your words is heightened by the childish scrawl they are written in, and I must work hard to fight back tears.

I thought so. We have written nearly identical lists.

- Stupid.
- Lazy.
- Ugly.
- Weird.
- Lonely.

I look up from the paper and you're still there, but you're about 15 now, sitting in a wheelchair not unlike my own. I see braces on your teeth as you hurry to cover your quivering mouth. I try to smile reassuringly and say, "You really feel like this. Still."

You quickly cast your eyes down to the ground and say to your shoes:

"Always."

You look back up at me. A single tear falls as if in slow motion from your right eye to the paper in your shaking hands. Clumsily and slowly, I find my way back from the floor into my wheelchair so that I can come close enough to you to gently brush your overgrown auburn fringe from your eyes.

"No," I say, "Not always. Look."

You take a deep, sniffly breath. You then sit in silence for a few minutes reading through my musings, which include not only a list of adjectives that don't describe you but also evidence of why people who have called you those things – mostly yourself – were sorely mistaken.

Stupid – Let's try and remove this word from our vocabulary altogether over time. Concepts like "stupidity" and "intelligence" are rooted in ableism and extremely rigid ideas of what makes a person clever or worthy. But you are clever, Kel. You are clever enough to have figured out from a very young age that something about you was very different, although you will not have the words (and diagnoses) to explain it until your twenties and thirties. I could try and explain it now, but I have been wondering if maybe we didn't learn those things until we were truly ready, so I won't ruin the surprise. Or perhaps it is more accurate to say I do not want to detract from the enormous relief and sense of self you are eventually going to discover. It's worth waiting for! Trust me.

You are clever enough to notice differences in the way other people think, act, and even how they speak, teaching yourself intuitively how to emulate speech patterns and behaviours that will make it easier for those people to understand you. Basically, this means that in a way you are clever enough to learn a new language without a single formal lesson, without a phrase book, and without even knowing exactly what the language is. That is pretty damn clever. My only regret about you using your cleverness in this way is that it often comes at the cost of your own comfort and happiness. Even from a young age, you instinctively knew that in order to fit in with others, you needed to push **out** certain natural behaviours and characteristics. You've pushed them out so far and so long that all these years later we are still trying to learn how to let them back into our life. Please know that I am not angry at you for this. I am so thankful that you did what you thought you needed to do to survive in this world until we were ready and safe enough to start thriving. It is your cleverness and insightful nature that has brought us to a place in life where thriving is finally possible. But please know that you were never unacceptable. The world was inaccessible to your true self, and one day all these experiences will help you change little corners of that world in some important ways.

Lazy – Imagine this little scene: a tortoise and a cheetah stand side by side at the starting line of a sprint race. Both creatures prepare themselves by stretching their bodies, fuelled by proper training and nourishment. However, as the starting pistol reverberates through the air, the cheetah launches forward with astonishing speed, leaving the tortoise trailing behind in a cloud of dust. But does this mean the tortoise is lazy? Absolutely not. It is a hardworking and capable creature in its own right, just as a tortoise should be. If it were to constantly compare itself to the cheetah and expect the same level of performance, it would only set itself up for failure and inevitable disappointment.

You, dear Kelly, are like that tortoise. Your disabled body and neurodivergent mind, with its beautiful, unpruned synapses flourishing like a wild garden, contribute to your unique strengths and challenges. Your focus can be remarkably intense, though it may not always be sustained for long periods, and your energy levels may deplete more rapidly than those of some others. It is crucial to understand that this is not a reflection of laziness on your part, Kelly. Rather, it is a manifestation of exhaustion. I implore you to embrace the idea of rest as an essential part of your advocacy, both for yourself and for others. By prioritizing your well-being and allowing yourself adequate time to recharge, you will become an even stronger advocate for the causes you hold dear. Remember, better health will serve as the foundation for your resilience and effectiveness in making a difference.

Ugly – Oh, little one. What could possibly be ugly about a body that defies the odds? Survival is always beautiful. Your body has already survived so much, and, although it may be difficult to believe right now, I promise that it will survive much more to come. Your body is just a house, and like the creak in your grandparents' old floorboards in Whyalla, your cracks and scuffs and chips are just signs of what you have withstood. Sure, we could probably stand to tidy our house a bit more often than we do. Eventually, when you start taking better care of yourself, you will find that what decreases the size of that pit in the bottom of your stomach little by little each time you look in the mirror is not the fact that you look different. It's because you **feel** different. Yes, cutting your hair more regularly will free your face from its obscurity, which will attract more compliments, but haircuts also achieve something else when it comes to you. Something far more important than praise or looking more conventionally attractive. Running your hands through your freshly buzzed undercut will provide you with a great deal of pleasurable self-stimulation (which you'll later learn is called "stimming" – something you do a lot of in different ways). The ability to be in a body that increasingly meets your sensory needs, instead of making you feel like you want to crawl out of your skin, will make you feel a peace that, ironically, hits you like a truck – a peace that you didn't previously know you were missing. That is what is beautiful, Kel. You are most beautiful when you are happy and peaceful enough to be grateful to your body for all it has endured and all it continues to give you.

Actually, while we are on the subject of being at peace with and in your mind and your body, there are some other things we should talk about…

You have already noticed by now that you are feeling attracted to certain people regardless of their gender or self-expression. Girls, boys, masculine girls, feminine boys and everything in between, as long as they radiate gentleness most of all. As a creative person, the varied and undulating landscape that is self-expression has always fascinated you. I know that right now, at the age you are when we are sitting together like this, it feels so daunting to realize this about your sexual and romantic identity. I know that this discomfort is intensified hugely by the fact that you don't yet have the words to describe it. And, not knowing that the right words and concepts to describe your feelings do actually already exist, you feel completely alone in this. You feel, once again like that round peg, willing to do anything just to spend five minutes in the correct hole so you can have a break from your mind's painful and exhausting insistence on being "different". But here's the thing. When it comes to sexuality, it turns out you really aren't that "different" after all.

I am very reluctant to quote an actual statistic here since statistics on identity-based topics can vary wildly depending on factors like personal definitions and how the questions are asked. For now, thanks to the work of some amazing advocates (some of which you have the honour of getting to meet and work alongside from time to time), people are becoming increasingly comfortable with identifying as queer just like you, as it thankfully becomes safer to do so. It is fascinating and beautiful the way that once people start judging other people less, they sometimes open themselves up to gently exploring their own selves with curiosity. And in this vein, as you explore uncharted corners of your own mind like a forgotten wing of a beautiful old library, you will find new information that makes your sense of your own gender shift a little bit, too. A word to the wise: let it happen. The more you fight against it or insist that you must fit neatly into one gender or another, the more painful it will become and the more that part of you will fight its way out to get addressed. Unanswered questions have always been one of your favourite things, so it's okay to let yourself be one sometimes.

Weird – You know what? I'm not actually going to rebut this one, just question your value judgement on it. Your weirdness is your creativity. It is what allows you to create entire worlds out of words and continually search for methods and perspectives that not only help you find a purpose in this overwhelming world but help others find their voice, too. Change is always weird. Without an appreciation for different ideas and perspectives, diseases would go uncured, black holes would go undiscovered, and women who had opinions would still be getting burned at the stake. Weirdness is an essential component of learning and progress. Keep using yours for good wherever and however you can.

Let me finish by saying that I hope all of the above proves to you that you will not always be lonely. Embracing your whole self, including your disabilities, has opened you up to a whole new world of opportunity and a close-knit little community of weirdos you can no longer picture your life without. In fact, at times you will find yourself feeling so accepted and loved that it is physically uncomfortable for you, as your body and heart learn to open up to feelings you always thought were for other people, not you. Evolution is uncomfortable, but much less so than staying the same while life leaves you behind.

Kelly, I wish you all the best discomfort this life has to offer. Know that I am still here for you, growing every day and learning bit by bit how to finally give you …

All my love,

Kelly

5
Zoe Simmons

Zoe Simmons writes to make a difference. As an award-winning journalist, copywriter, author, and speaker who's been published hundreds of times around the globe, Zoe uses the raw power of storytelling to capture hearts and minds. A fierce advocate for disability, mental illness, and chronic illness, Zoe speaks candidly about her experiences with fibromyalgia, undiagnosed adenomyosis, bipolar, anxiety, and autism. Through her work, she aims to smash stigma, create change, and show others they're not alone.

Having been published in six books, including this book, a section on ethical journalism in Kathy Divine's *Golden Age Politics*, five poems on chronic pain, mental health, disability, and discovering queerness in three Beyond The Veil Press mental health anthologies, and a chapter on how journalism helped her community in the bushfires in Occupational Therapy Australia's *Doing Our Best*, Zoe is currently writing her first book about being a disabled journalist – and her community's struggle for survival – in the 2019/2020 Black Summer Bushfires.

You can follow Zoe online on Instagram, TikTok, and Threads (@SomethingBeginningWithZ), Facebook (@ZoeSimmonsJournalist), or X (formerly known as Twitter) (@ItBeginsWithZ), or check out her website www.ZoeSimmons.com.au for more.

Zoe's story – Dear teenage Zoe

I'm not going to lie to you: growing up is going to be rough. You're autistic and bipolar, but you don't know that yet. And living with disabilities, you aren't aware of what will make existing in a non-disabled world so incredibly difficult – especially when you develop chronic pain and fatigue in your twenties.

You'll feel out of place a lot. You'll feel like you aren't enough. You'll feel like you should do and be more – and you'll also feel like you're just not supposed to be here. You'll feel guilty for existing. You'll wish with all your heart and soul that you could cease to exist, many times. But, even with every terrible thought you'll have, and every terrible thing that's going to happen, you will persist. And it will only make you stronger.

Thankfully, it won't be all bad. You'll see that even in the darkness there is always light. You'll see the beauty in the world, and fall in love with magic in the mundane, like the caress of an ocean breeze and the feeling of soft sunlight kissing your skin. You'll have some of the most incredible experiences, and you'll be so glad you stayed.

Because you'll learn how to transmute that darkness. You'll learn to take all the awful parts of life, and create them into something beautiful – through your writing, your journalism, your speaking, your poetry, and your advocacy. Yes, **speaking.** I know that might sound wild to you, considering public speaking assignments were almost always the ones that got you the worst marks, but don't beat yourself up about it. Because you'll actually become an excellent speaker for causes that you're passionate about, like disability. In fact, in the year I'm writing this, we've just been a keynote speaker at a national disability conference. It will be the first time you publicly talk about the fact that you're autistic, and you'll receive the most amazing feedback. It will make your heart glow.

And yes, we're a writer! We're also a poet, a journalist, and an author. We've even won awards for our work, and have been published in several books. Best of all, we're fighting to smash stigma through words and make the world a better place. We became everything the younger us needed. So please, keep fighting, because I promise: this too shall pass. And all your dreams are going to come true.

I wish I could tell you it will get easier. But the truth is: it won't. Because you're autistic, there's a lot about communication, socialization, and unwritten societal rules you won't understand. You're going to mask, a lot. You'll mask so well that you don't even realize you're masking: and it will utterly exhaust you. Being autistic will also mean that you won't see a lot of red flags. You're going to encounter a lot of awful people, many of whom will try to take advantage of you – and unfortunately, some of them will.

I'd tell you to watch out for them – like the so-called friends that play awful pranks on you and pretend to be your crush via email, but tell you your "relationship" needs to be a secret. Like the so-called friends who exclude you from group activities that involve your special interests – you'll find out because you call their mum, only to discover all your "friends" lied. And like the so-called ableist friends who will abandon you when you start developing an incurable nerve disorder – who believe you're the one who caused your chronic pain, and you could fix it if you just "tried harder" (yikes). But their actions say more about them than they do about you.

And one day, you'll barely remember their names.

But I know it's hard. I know that right now you're probably feeling so gut-wrenchingly lonely, and oh so low. I know you're probably wondering how you'll get through this. I know it feels hopeless, and you don't see a future. And I know you don't want to be here anymore, because I still bear those scars. Someday, we'll never pick up a blade again, and we'll cover those scars with pretty flower tattoos.

Being a teenager, especially one with undiagnosed disabilities and a complex mental illness, is so tough – but you're doing such a fucking good job. Just keep your head down, work hard, and keep holding on. You've got this, even if you don't feel like it.

These next few years will test you. Especially when, like sharks to blood, the bullies can sense you're different. They'll make fun of you, especially when you try to be yourself. They'll call you ugly, fat, weirdo, freak, loser, emo, and worse. They'll make you want to hide yourself. They'll make fun of your art. They'll mock your style and taste in music. They'll find you on social media and bully you relentlessly – including people you once considered your friends. They'll go into your locker and destroy your things, including your treasured *Twilight* poster. You'll watch the torn pieces blow away on the wind before you can catch them.

They'll hunt you like prey.

And because you're kind, you won't bite back in the way they deserve it. You'll just keep holding onto the thought that life has to be more than this – that you're meant for greater things: and you are. Success is the best revenge.

(But part of me also wishes we had the courage to tell a lot more people to fuck off.)

In case you need a reminder, your kindness doesn't make you weak. Your emotions don't make you weak. In fact, they make you stronger – and the fact that you feel **so much** and keep going and fighting for what you believe in is true strength. But it won't always feel like it.

Like when you stand up to a bully many years older than you who's making fun of your friends for being gay. She will punch you in the face and try to break your nose. She will threaten more violence. But that won't stop you. And you aren't alone. Your wonderful mum always has your back. She'll go to the police for you, and that bully will never touch you again.

And when you move suburbs away from the bully, you'll tell her: "next time you'll see me, I'll be on TV." You'll die a bit from the embarrassment of saying those words, but you also weren't wrong. A little over a decade later you **will** be on TV – multiple times, advocating about causes you care about. You don't even remember her name any more.

Your strong sense of social justice is a gift. But people will make fun of how passionate you are. They'll get annoyed with it, too. Whether it's about gender, sexuality, the environment, animal rights or disability. They'll tell you you're being dramatic, that you're overreacting, that you're too sensitive, and that nothing will ever change: but they are wrong. Even a single voice can change the world – or at least, someone's world. And your words will spark more change than you can imagine. Keep believing in a better world. Someone has to.

It might not seem like it now, but some day you'll look back and you'll be so proud of yourself. I know, because I'm 27-year-old Zoe, and I am filled with such gratitude to you. Because you made us who we are today. I would not be where I am without you, and I can't thank you enough for pushing through the muck and staying true to your heart, even when it's scary. I love you.

It does make me sad to look back and remember how we let people treat us, though. And I wish you wouldn't hate yourself as much as you do: you don't deserve it. I wish I could give you a big hug and tell you that you are worthy, and that everything will be okay. I wish you could see yourself how I see you: a young autistic person, doing their best to navigate a world that wasn't built for us. Someone who loves deeply, and always tries their best. Someone who is so goddamn brave, even when you're afraid. Someone who's quirky, caring, and – admittedly – a bit weird: but that is what makes you fantastic. Embrace it. Own it. Because by the time you're my age you'll realize it's a big part of what makes people love you. They'll see you for who you are – and help you realize that the nasty things your brain says about you aren't true.

Even so, you'll go through most of your life pretty much believing everyone hates you. You'll feel like you're walking on eggshells. You'll always do more, because you want them to love you. You'll want to prove you are worthy of love. But darling, you already are. And if anyone makes you feel like you are a burden or not enough, run. You do not owe them your love or your time.

Instead, give that love to yourself – because you are **wonderful.** And you will find your people who think **the world** of you.

It's like the Dr Seuss quote says: Be who you are and say what you feel. Because in the end, those who matter don't mind, and those who mind don't matter.

And they **don't** matter. Now, they're just words on a page.

High school – thank the goddess – does not last forever. Pretty soon, you'll be out of there. You'll move away from the small minds of a small town. You'll go to university and study journalism and philosophy. You'll encounter more bullies, but you will leave them behind too. And with hard work you'll graduate at the top of your class.

Life will keep throwing you curveballs. Your disabilities will get worse, even though you don't even know they're disabilities yet. You'll lose friends. You'll leave bad jobs. You'll get your heart broken, and people you love will die. That loss will hurt more than any other pain you've experienced. But life grows around the grief, and it will show you who is actually there for you – and it will remind you that life is short. We keep living, where they cannot.

And we'll get better at reading the signs, and realizing when things aren't good for us. Like the guy who comforts you for several months as a friend after your beloved Pop dies, but gets angry at you when you won't sleep with him. He'll go around calling you awful names, and you'll be so glad you didn't fall for his lies.

I wish I could stop some of the bad things that are coming. I wish I could have stopped some of the things that have already happened – the things that haunt us in our dreams. But I need you to know it's not your fault. None of it is. And you do not deserve the hatred that's been thrown at you. Especially the hatred that comes from within your own mind. Let it go, my love. Let it all go. You are worth so much more. You are so goddamn strong, and you will conquer every challenge that comes your way. Every scar will build your throne.

Life is full of so much bad, and so much good. And you'll experience all of it. From the grief and survivor's guilt of watching your hometown burn in the Black Summer Bushfires, and battling the medical system to be heard when you start developing fibromyalgia and adenomyosis, to the thrill of being published hundreds of times around the globe, and being internationally recognized for your writing and advocacy work.

And our story is still only just beginning.

One day, things will make so much more sense. You'll have more clarity. You'll be able to set boundaries (or at least, try to!). You'll let go of expectations, and what isn't right for you. You'll finally start to love yourself, as you dismantle the stories other people held for you. And it will be a huge thing when, at 27, you'll finally be diagnosed as autistic.

You'll realize so many of the challenges we faced were because of a neurotypical, heteronormative, ableist society. You'll learn about sensory issues, burnout, and how to look after yourself better. You'll start using mobility aids, which will get you a lot of weird looks and a lot of stigma as a young person: but they make life so much better, so don't let anyone ever make you feel bad about your freedom machines. You'll learn about your access needs, and you'll learn to stop feeling like a burden or a hassle because of them. You'll learn to rest – and also learn that you don't have to meet society's expectations. You don't have to force yourself into non-disabled boxes, especially when it harms you.

Be true to yourself. Because you will forge your own path.

You will find yourself. You will unapologetically take up space. And you will change the world.

So, no matter what you're feeling now, I want you to know there is always hope.

And even if you don't believe in yourself, I believe in you. Just like the future Zoe believes in me.

6
Dr Wenn Lawson

Dr Wenn is passionate about autism, mental health, all things LGBTQIA+ and building autism understanding across the generations, professions, and the world. He is a neurodivergent practitioner tutor for Birmingham University (UK), where he has worked for nearly two decades. Dr Wenn is an Adjunct Associate Professor with Curtin University, WA, and a member of CARG (Curtin University's Autism Research Group). He has published as a Senior Researcher with Macquarie University, Sydney, NSW, Curtin University, WA, and University of Queensland, Australia. Wenn's focus has been to highlight the need for co-production in a variety of neurodivergent research, to contribute to the call of the autistic voice – "it must be nothing about me without me" – and to highlight the needs of those who are late in coming to a recognition of their autism as well as the effect that adaptive morphing (masking) has had on mental health.

Wenn is a key theorist of the Monotropic theory of autism who is working with others to create understanding and support for Monotropism as a key characteristic of autism. Dr Wenn came forth in Victoria as Australian of the Year in 2008, presented on autism and ageing to the United Nations in 2017, and won the Lesley Hall Lifetime Achievement Award for Disability leadership in 2021. Wenn resides on a number of boards, including the editorial board for "Autism in Adulthood", the AARC (Australasian

Autism Research Council), the Autism Research Institute (ARI) (US), and The American Autism Association. As well as being a well-known author, Wenn is a family man with a love for birds.

Wenn's story – A letter to my teenage self

This chapter is about what I would have liked my much younger self to have known, so my journey through the teenage years might have been less confusing and less troubled.

Hi, my name is Wenn Lawson and I'm a neurodivergent trans guy. Before I tell you what I'd write in a letter to my teenage self, I want to give you some information about me. Currently I'm in my seventies, after being married and raising a family with four children, going through divorce, then marrying the love of my life and opting to live in my true gender. I have often wished I could have told my teenage self some of the things I know now. Of course, it's easier to offer advice when we can look back and view situations from wisdom gathered afterwards.

This chapter shares some of those things. There are other things that I'm aware of now that I wasn't aware of as a teenager. For example, I don't think I "masked" (tried to hide my true self by mimicking others and trying to fit in with my peers) who I was very well, or even understood that concept. But I know this is an issue for many. I didn't have a correct diagnosis or recognition of my autism until I was an older adult (age 42), so I lived with lots of confusion about myself and the world I was part of. I knew I didn't "fit" with others of my age and it was uncomfortable being around my peers. I just didn't know why.

I spent many years coming to terms with who I am, why I am, and what being me means. I didn't have access to the knowledge I now have so I wasn't able to use such knowledge at the time of being a teenager. But first I'll share with you some of my experiences as a teenager, so you can get more insight into some of the context.

For me, memories of being a teenager are vivid and hard to erase. Before my thirteenth birthday, I'd spent almost a year in an orthopaedic hospital with a serious bone disease (osteomyelitis) that impacted my left tibia (the smaller of the two main long bones in the lower leg). I was first diagnosed with osteomyelitis aged ten, back in November 1962. After my eleventh birthday, in February 1963 (still in hospital), I was given the opportunity to "sit" for my eleven-plus exam. I was the only child in a barren room with a desk and chair. I was told to sit at the desk, on the chair, but not to turn the paper over until I was told to. Then, after a few moments, I was told to turn the paper over and write my name at the top. I did so. Then I sat at that desk, on that chair, until I was told I could leave. No one told me to answer the questions on the paper, only to write my name. I was pretty bored sitting there but I laid my head on my arms and snoozed on and off, until I was told I could go.

Although I didn't have a diagnosis back then, I struggled to learn in the traditional ways. My school reports told of how I was easily distracted, not good at doing as I was told, and was often in trouble (usually for things I had no idea about). I didn't "pass" my eleven-plus exam.

Anyway, getting back to being in the hospital, where we had daily school lessons, and I was part of a ward with 20 children...

life was pretty much insulated from the outside world. Before my twelfth birthday I was discharged from hospital. I needed to wear a full-length leg iron (calliper) on my left leg as it had been in a cast for almost a year. I had had a large amount of diseased bone removed from it and it just wasn't strong enough to hold my weight on its own. I also walked with crutches, and after six months I eventually used a walking stick.

Upon leaving hospital and travelling in my dad's car I remember being in awe of the large billboards in the town carrying various advertisements. I had never seen these before. I also wasn't used to noisy traffic, crowds of people, and the everyday demands of life outside the hospital.

Going to an all-girls high school at the age of 12 was an utter nightmare. At the best of times, I felt like an outsider around females and I had no idea of how to behave. I didn't join in the physical games during school PE because of my weak leg but also because I couldn't relate to them and I had no interest.

I began menstruation aged ten, but it always felt like my period crept up on me and I was taken by surprise!

Turning 13 and officially becoming a teenager didn't help matters either. I simply didn't understand the world around me or within me. I lived with frequent headaches and dizzy spells, sore breasts or nipples and a seeming "other life" within my body that was causing it to change, but without my consent.

No one explained to me what I might expect from being a teenager, whether that was about getting my monthly period, physically changing as my breasts and body hair grew, or what might happen when various hormones tore their way through my body. I remember trying to stay flat-chested, covering up my body with clothing that was a bit big for me, and trying to fly beneath the radar (not get noticed) around other young people.

Eventually I found some work for a few months with an animal park. I lived about five miles away from the park (in Somerset, UK) and cycled there each day. My duties involved being responsible for a young brown bear called Bruin, the Pet's Corner (which housed rabbits, guinea pigs, and some other young animals), a porcupine, and some fallow deer.

I was able to work there between leaving school at the age of 15, in July of 1967, and going off to college in September of that year. College was in a different town to where I lived. The animal park was called "Longleat" and I absolutely loved it!

Eventually, I settled into a daily routine of being a student at college, where I studied a "pre-nursing" course and obtained my GCEs (high school certificate with "O" levels) and two "A" levels in English and English Literature. I found a local church fellowship and joined the youth group there, as well as joining a local Church of England bell-ringers' group. I didn't go home very often, just for some longer holidays in the summer, because I loved being able to make my own choices and not have to comply with parental ideology. My parents ran a "working men's club" in Kent during my college years but I didn't have a bedroom in their house, so when I visited them, I slept on the couch in the lounge. They didn't approve of my "Christian" theology and it was uncomfortable not feeling "accepted" for who I was at that time.

For a teen such as myself, being a teenager in the mid to late sixties had a heap of difficulties. I wasn't fully disabled by my previous "leg" issues, but I also wasn't fully able either. I often had pain in my left leg and used a walking stick intermittently. I also struggled with my studies and found it hard to listen to a lecture and take notes. I didn't have an assessment of any specific learning difficulty, but it was understood that I was probably dyslexic and dyspraxic (had issues with writing, spelling, reading, and movement co-ordination). These issues were later confirmed in my mid-adult years.

Looking back on those years now from where I am today, I understand so much of my confusion and what it means to be a neurodivergent person with learning difficulties (dyslexia, dyspraxia, and dyscalculia). Of course, it's always easier to "see" through the fog when looking back and after the fog has lifted.

If I had to visit those years again (I wouldn't want to live there) I'd hope I could utilize some of the knowledge I have today. To help me sort this out in a way that aids understanding, I'm going to use some headings.

Becoming a teenager, or early adolescence

When I became a teenager I was told that I wasn't a child anymore and it was expected that I could manage more things on my own. The trouble was, I couldn't. I had no comprehension of time, space, and place or of how to get to places. I was OK if I knew where to wait for a particular bus or train and would try to stay with what I knew. If I got lost, I used to ask for directions. This was problematic because I often got told conflicting things or I couldn't hold the instructions in my head or I put myself at risk by talking to a stranger.

Becoming a teenager is preparation for parting with childhood while not yet able to enter adulthood. It will mean joining a new tribe and there is an expectation that, as such, I would be learning how to harness my emotions. The problem is, no one explains things to you. At least, they didn't explain anything to me.

There is also an understanding (apparently) that I would be able to separate adult authority from my peers, and begin to build a future that would enable me to plan for adulthood. But this was never explained to me. Then there is all the information about a developing sexuality, relating to peers, and separating romantic friendships from those that are platonic. On top of all of this I was supposed to be learning about personal hygiene and how to care for myself!

The letter

Dear Wenn,

I'm writing you a letter because I am much older now and I want to share with you some of the things that I now know would have been useful to understand when I was a teenager. I know you are going through some tough times at the moment and life feels very confusing. School is really tough on you and there is an expectation that you will know what is expected of you each day. Although it is difficult to get a handle on things such as remembering your schoolbooks, finding your way around school, and getting to things on time, I want you to know that you can ask for support. Please make an appointment with the head teacher and share with them your concerns. It's OK to feel confused and worried that you are going to get things wrong. It's absolutely fine to let the school know you need support. They might find you a peer who knows the school and the timetable better and can act as a guide for you. They might set up a staff meeting with all of your teachers so you only have to tell everyone once that you need help.

> Autism is: I like it here, please do let me stay.
> Autism is: I know it here, please don't take
>   me away.
> If and when I leave this place to travel to
>   another space,
> I need to know it right away. I need to know that
>   I'm OK.
> Transition is so fleeting, it leaves not time to stay.
> Will I have time to settle, or will I be whisked away?
>
> I know that change can happen.
> I know it can take time.
> But how can I know what this will mean?
> What this will mean for mine.
> Transition is about moving, "to where or what"
>   one asks?
> This is my very question, from present or the past.
> Time for me is all the same,
> I know not of its future.
> I only know I trust in "now"… tomorrow can come,
>   I just need to know how.

I remember thinking: Why don't people say what they mean? "You have to go to school now", for example. They don't say, "school now but later you will come home again". Every day I left my home, my room, not ever knowing if I would return.

Putting some structure into your day will be very helpful. You could write it down in your diary, or on your iPad or phone. You could use your "Smart watch" to remind you of things you need to do, whether it's about homework (school work you do at home) or the time for eating and going to bed.

If we structure our day it's like putting up the scaffolding that supports us as we meet the demands of the day.

> Communication, orchestration and any
>   other "ation",
> Can lure and connive its path
> On people's thoughts and others' behalf.
> But what of us autistics?
> We think and we ponder,
> While you lot sit and wonder.
> "What is exactly going on?"
> You say within your mind.
>
> We know without a doubt.
> But you need time to work it out.
> For us it's all so simple!
> Words are what they seem to be.
> To us there is no problem!
>
> Herein lies the hitch you see,
> Words for you or words for me?
> We tend to
> view things
> differently!

Being autistic and feeling so different to others is absolutely normal for us, even though it's uncomfortable. The discomfort might make you want to cover up your difference and try to mimic what other people are doing. The problem is that living in denial of who you are and trying to be someone else is exhausting and, over time, we run out of energy and can even develop anxiety that leads to "burn out". Instead of trying to be like everyone else, we could find others who are like us and build our own community. There might be someone at school or there might not be, but conforming and pushing ourselves into a shape that isn't us is soul-destroying.

Maybe, Wenn, as you are good at poetry and stories, you could join a writer's club or a book club. I know you love to read, especially fantasy and science fiction books. Being with others who are also interested in the same things would really help you feel "less alone".

I remember when I heard the words from the PE teacher:

"…Wenn, aren't you changed yet?" I felt scared. What was I to become? What might I change into? What and when might this change occur? Would it be a sudden change? How do we work out group interaction unless the processes are explained?

Wenn, lots of teenagers feel this way. It's OK to need support and to ask for help. I know, Wenn, how literal you can be.

> So this is me!
> Twiddle dee and twiddle dum,
> How on earth have I begun?
> I started out all right you see,
> But now I question "who is me?"
> Which of these I know so well,
> How I wish that I could tell.
> If only it could stay the same,

I'd work the rules out for this game.
They call the movie "Life" you see,
But which is them and which is me?
I know for me the words serve well,
But as for others, who can tell?
I thought I'd got it,
But then came the shock.
You lot knew it,
But I did not!!

Not knowing what to say or what to do is a horrid feeling. I know you are very anxious about this. But let your good friend know about those bits you find hard, then you can discover the way through the maze together.

I know how pressured you feel when there is an expectation to do something within a specific time. It actually makes it even more difficult to focus and/or remember stuff. Consequently, you often get to school or wherever without your reader, PE kit, diary, and suchlike. I know getting yourself organized is very difficult for you, but there are ways to get around this.

Hey Wenn, you could use structure to assist you with this. You could request structured outlines from others too. You could make lists, use your computer as a diary to record events and appointments, check in with others about plans and expectations, and aim to have a number of strategies for the "but if…" events.

I know, Wenn, how hard it is to relate to others. The other teenagers in your class seem to know how to talk to each other and understand one another and they don't seem to have any problem with reading "body language" to gauge people's intentions or notice any change in their mood. For you, Wenn.

7
Empress Eyrie

The goddess of badass.

Mountain landscapes rise like the curve of her hips, her breath is the warm air of summer, her skin as smooth as quartz crystals. She is the serenity of the rainforest, but just as dark, wild, and untamed. A walking art gallery she wears her skin like a canvas and her heart on her sleeve. The Empress can fill you with the world's beauty, if you just let her in…

Sometimes strange, sometimes sensual, sometimes both, Empress Eyrie blends burlesque with performance art and storytelling to bring her soul to stages all over Australia. Empress adores travelling to perform and share her creations with audiences anywhere she can. She puts the dynamite into dynamic disability; able to do a cartwheel one day and not even put on her socks the next.

Empress is the proud owner and teacher at Tease-Able Burlesque School, the world's first disability owned and focused burlesque school. She prides herself on making burlesque open and accessible for everybody and adores being able to perform with her mobility aids and show the world that disabled people can be sexy and deserve to be seen.

An experienced artist, proud disabilibabe and all-round magical creature, there is nothing routine about her routines.

Make way for the Empress …

Empress' story – Dear younger self

No, I have to be honest here.

To a Version of Myself that I Barely Remember –

To a Version of Myself that Other People Remember Better Than I Do.

Trauma is a funny thing like that. It takes you. It shapes you. It becomes you.

I don't know when you'll get this. It could be you've got some tough times ahead. It could be that you're wasted from the tough times behind. Or – shit – it might be that you're in the thick of it right now.

I wish I could write something heartfelt, thinking back to specific moments that changed things. But the moments that do remain are either traumatic or frivolous.

I don't remember you. But I wish I did. But you are like a glimmer on the horizon, a flash deep in the mirrors that you see from the corner of the eye. You're not a tangible memory, more a concept. But now, now I feel real, well, almost, getting there.

What **is** it when people don't know or don't think of the event that shaped your entire being?

Like abuse. To me it has formed all we are. The reactions, the perceptions, the… everything! But to others it was a non-event or something that is easily forgotten in time or that they were never even told about. How can the universe be so nonchalant with that? The way we stick in others' minds and time stands still.

The worst time of my entire life, when everything broke apart. To them, just regular days, regular weeks, regular years.

It's shadowed over any good memories.

I can't say otherwise. I don't want to lie to you. I've had too much practice at that. I'm sorry.

But…

But…

It ironically becomes the things that make you find yourself. Force you.

There's one thing from you I remember clearly. One constant. Something I know has been a part of you – of us – since we took our first step. To step **out**, to step onto a stage.

You've always wanted to be on stages. To be a singer, an actor. Anything.

You love performance, and so do I.

Is it because you want to take some kind of control? To escape? Is it just that we love the idea of creating and showing off? Spoiler: all of the above.

You're good. That's OK. It's still in us.

But shit, I never thought I'd be writing the words, "I'm a burlesque artist from the future".

One thing I can't prepare you for is the shock of those around you now. Those who haven't seen you since you were an able-bodied kid running around and being wild. It's hard to try and explain an illness that has no explanation – even though it's one that I'm so used to. The sympathy feels weird, unnecessary. Worn out. Like,

I'm fine. I mean I'm not, we're not. We're painfully disabled – but I don't want to feel bad. And I don't.

Being an able-bodied youth. Well, teenager? Young person. Traumatized young person. (Whenever you are, you're way too young to have this much PTSD.) Things being as they are, I don't know how to prepare you for just how much pain you will endure. Mental and physical. I don't want to burden you. So yes, now we use a walking stick or a rollator (What? A rollator. It's like a Zimmer frame with wheels. What's a—? Look, you're always in the library, go look it up), sometimes even a wheelchair. I can't really say I ever thought about being disabled. Hardly anyone does. I always say I don't really have any regrets, but I still wish you'd had the education to understand what would happen to us.

I'm so sorry.

This will progress as the years go on, but that's not the end of the world. In fact, it opens up an entirely new one. Filled with… well, is it a horrible cliché to say "filled with wonder"? But it will be. We find something that is brighter and better than you can imagine. Interesting people. New **genuine** friendships, people who **honestly** like you, who actually **want** to be around you, who understand you. And you understand them. Well, some of them. People are still people, whenever and wherever we are.

This is the shock. It's hard to explain to you now, but you'll have **actual human beings** who love you. Not just people who deign to be near you until the bell rings.

Not just people. All those things I mentioned? Those things we loved fall to the wayside, but they come back: performance, music, art, dance, and creation. They never really go away. The things that always kept you sane, kept you here, have become your lifeblood. Your everything. We'll come back to those, but it's true, so many of them suffered from years of being put away but you'll need that time for staying alive, that's more important. But it's never too late to get it all back. To re-find your joys.

Love isn't as hard as it will feel when it finally finds you, and I'm sorry for what you have to go through to get there. We'll find a day when we have a deep love and a beautiful family. I feel honestly, deeply lucky. Which may feel like a strange thing to say, given just how much it hurts or how much I've been through. But I do, not because I'm disabled – fuck. (Yeah, the potty mouth doesn't improve.) I'd be happy not to have this – but two things can be true at once; I am also grateful for the community and friends I have managed to find. The pride in myself, the absolute bliss. I have felt so much joy in teaching and learning and opening my soul to audiences and to myself.

Occasionally a good memory comes back. And it makes me realize that this life, the life I live now, is not far from the life I always wanted. But never expected.

Everything hurts, but I wouldn't trade it for not being me. This me.

"This me"? Right. Let me tell you about a book you're gonna read. Chill, I'm not gonna ruin it. It's OK, it's a good one.

It's called *Witches Abroad* by Terry Pratchett (Pratchett, 2013). Great book, one of my faves, but I'll sum up this one bit for you. There's a mirror realm that traps a pair of sisters. They see reflections of reflections, images, and images of themselves, thousands and thousands of times over. Death tells them that to get free, they have to pick which of the thousands of themselves is their real self. You can get driven mad, get overloaded, trying to guess. But when one of the sisters, one of our leads, gets stuck there, sees all the hers, and gets asked which self is real, she just ignores all the other images, looks down at her own self and says, "*This* one."

That's who I am. That's who we are. So many selves I've been, so many selves I am. The artist, the abuse survivor, the show-off, the mother, the child, the teacher, the pregnant teenager, the cripple, the performer, the lover, the fool, the Empress. Which is the real me? **I** am.

Sometimes I feel that **I've** stepped through a mirror. Like the youth that I was never existed. But you did. You do. You're my real self too. Even though I don't always have the memories of you.

For years we ran, we ran until we couldn't run any more. We broke ourselves running. Just stop. When you stop, you find yourself – when you stop running and actually see yourself.

Remember what I said before? About how performance gives us a control, gives us an escape? Each time I step (or roll) onto a stage with an audience watching I am in control; it's the one time the world stands still, just for me. I hold power; it's not taken away from me by my trauma or the people who hurt me, or by my body or my pain. It's mine. I own it. It's the power that we didn't feel, that was taken away so, **so** many times in so many ways.

One of the best bits now? I don't care if I don't always have control up there. I just want the experience and the joy. There's a lot between there and here, but it's coming. You'll be able to experience joy… just for the sake of joy. You don't need to feel guilty for it. You don't need to "earn" it. You can be happy about something… and just be happy about it. And just be **happy**.

By the way, you give yourself a gift to take up there. A name. Empress. I know, right? Yep, it's from the Tarot. That card's already started to follow you, and it won't quit. So, we embrace it. Now it's an energy that you embody, that you strive for. Once you're on that stage or in front of that camera, everyone there, every soul watching, they're there for you, and you for them. You share your thrill, giving it and receiving it.

Live that joy, feel that joy. If the universe offers you happiness, don't be weird about it – just take it.

I remember when a doctor told me, "I have little old ladies with better hips than you". It made me realize things were never gonna be the same. That I'd lost that part of my life where everything functioned. I'd lost a life where I wasn't in pain.

I didn't want to be here anymore.

I didn't want to be **anywhere** any more.

Life forced me to live.

I'm glad it did.

I so wish you had been shown that support when you needed it. But you have it now, trust it.

You are allowed to just exist. I give you permission.

Live.

Love,

You

PS: Don't worry, we eventually get that curly hair under control. But the ultrasound gel that Mum brought home after her night shift at the hospital? The one that's stashed in the back of the bathroom drawers? It's **not** the answer, babes. Real products are, but we get there.

8
Emma Goodall

Emma Goodall (PhD) is an autistic author, researcher, parent, and senior public servant. Emma is passionate about improving day to day life as well as longer-term outcomes for neurodivergent folk.

Emma's story

Dear teenage me,

Don't worry, once you get through this stage of life, things will get easier. You will find lifelong friendships in both the queer community and the disability community. You know how you were so confused when the girls at school said you were a lesbian and then Vicky said that what you and her were doing made you a lesbian. I was so proud of you for not being ashamed of your sexuality. Even though life proved time and time again that in reality your sexuality is a lot more fluid than you thought and much more related to how people connect with you than what their genitals are.

In your last year at high school you will connect to the queer community at a time when people are still getting attacked and raped for who they choose to have sex with. You will start to heal from those non-consensual experiences that teenage boys inflicted on you, learning from gay men that it can be much easier to just leave the past in the past and focus on the now and sometimes the future. As a young adult, attending university, you will use your new massage therapy qualification to cement your kindness and compassion through volunteering to provide AIDS patients with a massage once a week. Ignore the bigotry and fear that emanates from other people when you idiotically tell them this. Instead, rest assured that by the time you are middle-aged, AIDS is no longer feared and people understand that you can't catch it from touching someone.

You will, however, have lived through huge amounts of sorrow and distress as mostly gay men die in huge numbers from AIDS. This will stand you in good stead for when Mike dies and you howl at your stupidity for not talking to him for three years after you both went for your first sexual health check-ups together. Your loss was compounded by only having reconnected with him once he was settled with a boyfriend who was stable and relatively good for him. Except, like many in the queer community in those days, Mike had never stopped self-medicating and spent his days and nights in a fog of alcohol and marijuana. Believe it or not, this becomes less and less common over the years as being queer becomes more acceptable and less stigmatized.

You will experience civil unions and gay marriage across Europe and Australasia being celebrated with genuine love and happiness with friends, family, whānau, and venue staff. You will find that the disability community is more accepting of queer folx than the queer community is of disabled people. You will walk alongside people as they explore their neurology, gender, and sexuality. The natural acceptance and celebration of your sexuality that you had at 16 will stand you in good stead to help educate others about the difference between healthy and unhealthy relationships. But only after you have experienced both. You will use your mistakes to educate others in the neurodivergent community by explicitly talking about the signs of healthy and unhealthy relationships and what to do when a relationship is becoming abusive.

You will discover that homophobia places barriers in the way of your career for years until, magically, one day no one seems to care if educators are queer or not any more. Sadly, at this point life will place some more career barriers in your way as ableism rears its ugly self. No longer willing or able to hide your autism, you will instead choose to be strong and reflective. "Why would you want to work for a company that isn't inclusive and welcoming?" The right job will come along at some point. You will find not just acceptance in the workplace, but deep understanding and respect for your skills and knowledge, vindicating the years of homophobia and/or ableism.

I wish I could tell you, my teenage self, that one day it will be safe to go wherever you want, whenever you want, but that day has not yet come. I can tell you that the seemingly ridiculous rape prevention advice that policemen gave the class when we were 15 will come in useful. So it is good you listened, even though you thought it was stupid.

I want to tell you about a couple of highlights in life that are coming your way.

One day you will hire a neurodivergent trans man, with a brilliant mind. You admire this man and want to ensure he feels welcomed in the team. You will send out one of his journal articles and a little blurb about his achievements and skills. You do not mention he is trans, only that he is male, because you feel that it is not your business to share. He gets to be fully accepted as a male and as a skilled and valuable individual by most people in the wider office. You are able to shield him from the few people who are ableist, even though they are ableist to you too. This brings both of you much joy.

One day, you will marry your girlfriend of over 12 years, ten years after your civil union. You will have the most amazing day, full of love, laughter, and joy. The room will be filled with neurodivergent and/or queer people, as well as the odd neurotypical and/or straight cisgender person. The venue staff will tell you that this is the best wedding they have ever held. You will forever fondly remember your niece throwing Lego during the speech her father gave. There were chairs on the dance floor for those people whose abilities meant they couldn't dance on their feet, headphones for those who were noise-sensitive, and sparkly lights, plenty of sparkly lights.

Your love of shiny, sparkly lights and soft, fluffy fabrics will be a source of great comfort and joy to you over the years. The soft blanket gifted to you in memory of your wife, when she died less than two years later, by a kind and caring lesbian couple, keeps your grief manageable at times. The love of those you love keeps it manageable the rest of the time. When Mike died you had so few friends; lost in finding yourself, you howled alone for three days solid. Now, you have friends who will support you whenever you need them; queer, straight, neurodivergent, etc.

You will love the son that came into your life as a 12-year-old. You will love him so much that you will learn that people who claim that a biological connection is needed to love a child properly have no idea what they are talking about. He will love you, not in spite of your autism but because of it. You will love him because he is who he is, quirky and kind, autistic and caring. You will love your friends so much that you will discover that there is no such thing as love being only for one person. You will learn that love is so much more than the English definitions; that the te reo Māori concept of *aroha* speaks to your heart and opens you up to so much more love in the world.

I will leave you, my teenage self, with the reflection that you are too hard on yourself and your parents at this stage in your life. The future you will realize that teens do not come with a manual and that neurodivergent teens don't fit the popular media solutions. You will become more thoughtful and compassionate, accepting that you, your parents and most people do the best they can with what they have got at any given point in any given day. You will listen to your son as he moves into adulthood in that stop, start, reverse, lurch forward way in which we neurodivergent people grow up. You will not judge him as you judged yourself, as you are content now, understanding that you are good enough now and that you were always good enough, even when feeling like you were drowning in mistakes and anxiety and ableism. You don't yet know that you are autistic; you just know you are different. And although you do a good act of pretending you are smarter than everyone else, you spend most of your time confused by everyone else. As an adult you will be surrounded by others who think like you or appreciate how you think, and this removes a lot of the confusion. What confusion remains is simply accepted. People are mysterious and they do confusing things, but it's OK. You can seek to understand when you are comfortable in your own skin around others. You will have grown into yourself and your self-acceptance and your self-worth. This will all be tempered with kindness and compassion, as you accept that this is who you are and if people choose to be mean to you or about you, that is a them problem, not a you problem.

Lots of love from your older and possibly wiser self, but mostly just your more confident and self-accepting self.

9
Freya Pinney

Freya Pinney, aka The Process Repository, is an autistic artist exploring concepts around identity and their relationship to the body. As a lesbian, her work also engages with and explores gender, sexuality, history, and critical theory and processes these themes across multiple media – from textiles to painting, sound, video, performance, sculpture, and writing creative non-fiction. She has been exhibiting art since 1995 in group and solo shows in SE Queensland, around Australia and in Japan, the UK, and the US. With a BA in Visual Arts with Honours from QUT and an MA in Fine Arts by research from QCA, Griffith University, she currently works as a Neurodivergent Affirming Art Therapist within an LGBTQIA+ company, while completing postgraduate studies at MIECAT. She has published on Neurodivergent Affirming Therapeutic Arts Practice within the *Journal of Creative Arts Therapies*, Australia. Her artwork can be seen on the cover of the Australian Federal Government Attorney-General Department's Disability and Mental Health Action Plan 2022–2025. Freya Pinney also does autism advocacy and presentations on neurodivergent affirming art therapy, including supporting sensory needs, valuing neurodiversity in the workplace, and using art with autistic children experiencing trauma. She has been instrumental in creating changes within Queensland Health, ensuring annual disability training for nurses at her local hospital, and statewide policy and administrative changes improving patient care and rights.

Freya's story – Hidden in plain sight

So strong. So thoughtful. So overwhelmed.

So tired. So on.

So careful. So creative. So brave.

Always watching, listening, following, adjusting self

Self-monitoring, hypervigilant, not trusting, and self-sacrificing

Always in a state of becoming, never feeling like I'm living

Living with a feeling of terror on the inside without any overt threat that was definable or communicable.

Words for my younger self...

My disability, like my sexuality, isn't something you can see ... unless you know what to look for. As a teen I was often silent and observed very closely. Once I had assessed every nuance I could then engage through incredible performances of well-crafted social roles. I was a master of disguise and had done theatre training since I was six, so I was adept at playing roles. I also didn't often know who I was underneath. I tried out several ways of "being" through my adolescence. I literally wore white face paint and heavy black eyeliner outside of school hours for years. Nothing like wearing a literal mask. But I also grew huge hair I could hide behind and crafted skills that negotiated social settings for me. In my twenties I engaged in experiments I called camouflage, where I dressed in different styles and went out in public to see if I could blend in. For example, I dressed in office clothes and went and stood in the city mall and had someone take photos and video of me from a distance. I was looking to see if I blended in and disappeared. I was conscious of these acts of camouflage being performances in costume, rather than attempts at trying to fit in. I love that I did this and have these memories. Growing up, I filled my social calendar with extra-curricular activities and copied others if ever in unstructured social settings.

I played the flute. But I didn't just play the flute. I had lessons at school as well as a private flute teacher and small group lessons with a music school. I played the flute in the school concert band, the school orchestra, the school wind ensemble, the weekend orchestra, the weekend wind ensemble, at functions organized by my flute teacher (e.g., art gallery openings, weddings, and funerals), etc. I had three sets of lessons a week as well as up to six group rehearsals – at school, after school, and on the weekend. In senior high school I also added the school musical band. That now seems a lot and requires some deep breaths to recover from even remembering that much. But… I also did drama at a theatre company, was in the school debate club, was the lighting director for the school junior musical, ran the school environment club, was on the state committee for the, performed in the school musicals, sang in the school vocal group that won our inaugural Queensland academy of music category award… AND… went to school.

I was anxious and quite terrified most of the time. I learned to feel the fear and do it anyway from a young age. I do not think this is always a good idea.

My mother was amazing. I only learned in my early forties that she parented my sister and me quite differently. I always assumed all parents spent hours talking through how their child's day went and dissecting interactions with teachers, then role-playing scenarios and conversations. Our nightly routine helped me process my days and work through my anxieties about tomorrow and included guided relaxation from my mum before she sang me to sleep. Every night. When I was older (teens and early twenties) I played relaxation music or nature sounds to go to sleep. I'm pretty sure my sister got a hug and "I love you" and a "good night". It takes an incredible human to parent so differently without either child knowing or feeling differently parented. My sister and I knew we were different but not in any significant way. My mother must have been exhausted.

One thing I found odd that my mother said to me was that being fat doesn't matter when it comes to love or sex. I would never have started a conversation on this topic with anyone ever when I was growing up. I have been fat since I was around four and I have felt body shame for as long as I can remember. I never changed my clothes in front of anyone. I used the toilet cubicle to change for school swimming. I didn't let anyone, including lovers, see me naked for years and I am still not comfortable being naked. As I recall, my mother gave me this strange piece of advice out of the blue. She was right. It was good advice. But I was horrified. I am pretty sure she told me just around the time I moved away from home. It was her life advice. I now wish I had asked questions, discussed it, and heard the stories that led to her sharing this randomly with me. I am pretty sure I actually said something like, "OK then" and then got on with what I was doing. It felt like it was something she wished someone had told her. Something it took her time to work out and that if someone had told her then it might have changed something about her. And this is a beautiful way of imparting lived experience.

So here are my things I have kind of worked out along the way but wish I'd had the insight to ask about if I'd realized these were actual things…

Sexuality is different to sexual preference

Sexuality for me is about how you feel about yourself and express yourself in terms of intimate pleasure. How you identify – your sexual identity. And identity is so interesting because it is not contingent on behaviour, but on the relationship that behaviour has with your sense of self and personhood. Many people have discrepancies between what they do with their bodies and how they identify their sexuality. And this can be individually, culturally, and socially determined, and historically contextualized. Sexuality also often changes over time. Growing up I didn't really think about my sexuality. I assumed I would want to date boys. I did date boys/men, but I didn't understand human relationships. I felt no connection romantically and I really just wanted to practice doing all the things I was supposed to so I could be normal. Literally. I wanted to "go out with" someone because I thought I was supposed to. But then I had no idea of what I was supposed to do or even want to do when "going out with" someone. My mum called it "going nowhere with" someone. I thought that it was important, but I didn't have any feelings about it. There was certainly no link between me and my sexuality in my adolescence.

When I lost my virginity, I was simultaneously so relieved and terrified. I actually thought that the reason he wanted to sleep with me was my outfit, so I made sure to wear the same clothes every time I saw him. There was nothing about pleasure involved in that transaction for me. Sex with men was just like "going nowhere with" someone. It was something I should do to be normal. When I realized at the age of 19 that I had a boyfriend and he had feelings for me, I completely freaked out. I suddenly saw the giant chasm between our perceptions of sexuality and I felt completely awful that I did not reciprocate his feelings. But I had deep feelings for a woman I knew. I found her intoxicating and saw her as untouchable and to be admired. I thought if she knew I had feelings for her I would be rejected, tainted, and worthless. I once heard her express her liking for a man we mutually knew. That was why I had slept with that man who, I'd just realized, had become my boyfriend and had feelings for me, but I was sleeping with him because the woman I desired liked him. So very drunkenly one night that I barely remember something magical happened with this woman. And I found my sexuality. She made me realize who I was. I was a lesbian. I romantically and sexually enjoyed the company of women. Not her, as I idolized her and was way too shy and self-conscious to have a relationship with her. I was interested in women sexually rather than men. I am a lesbian. My sexual preference was women. But it still took a little time for me to embrace being a lesbian as my identity.

Sexuality was still something I took ages to work out. I had worked out that I preferred women, great. But my sexuality and confidence in my body has taken far longer. By 21 I identified as a lesbian and I started my first lesbian relationship at 22. It was 20 incredible years of love and growing together with someone. Through that journey my sexuality changed many times. I experienced vast periods of asexuality and severe sensory aversion to touch, both of which were extremely hard for my partner at the time. She also lives with disabilities and we at times played the role of carer for one another. This definitely made things easier, but we were not always compatible in terms of sexuality and sexual preference, despite sharing a deep romantic love for one another. There were many times I felt how unfair it must have been on her. However, my sexual preferences did change over time (despite my lesbian sexual identity remaining intact) and our love was unwavering for two decades. And my mother was right – my obese body never impacted my ability to give or receive pleasure or love.

You can be friends with classmates or workmates but you have to make friends with them; it is not implied by the time you spend in the same place, and there is no formula for making friends.

I still struggle with this. And it still hurts me emotionally when I realize that people I thought were my friends are not. The line between friends and acquaintances is so blurry. How some people seem to have this as a boundary I may never understand. I still tend to overshare or under-share. But I can never tell if anyone else actually likes me. In social situations I seem to go on autopilot. It's like I play the role of social Freya and if people seem to smile, maybe laugh, and look happy then I have successfully created the identity of friend Freya (identity as outlined by Goffman, 1959). Yes, I just described masking and the constriction of my social identity through sociological references to the successful performance of a social role.

I have often opted for structured social engagements throughout my life. Activity groups, social clubs, political organizations, classes, social media groups, etc. Experiences where spending time with others is based on working towards a common goal. Within these groups I often gravitate towards organizing events, helping, or performing tasks. This structures my interactions with others and gives me defined social roles to play. But it also creates an assumption of camaraderie between me and others that may not be genuine for them.

When someone shares something personal with me, I usually overshare back something about myself. I do this in an effort to show that I care and they are not alone in having that experience. I am not intending to take away from their experiencing in any way but to foster a connection between us as people with deep experiences. I have learned over time to articulate this intention and that others do not always do this. I still feel uncomfortable asking others about their experiences as I feel like I am prying, even if they initiated sharing. My natural tendency is to offer more details about my own story in the hope they too will offer to share more with me. I find this concurrent sharing to be highly successful with other autistic people, but it is often not well received by neurotypical people. I have learned over the last seven years that my way of being, socially interacting, sharing, and communicating is completely normal for my neurotype. And that I prefer socializing with people who accept and understand me. I find myself often telling people I am autistic. It is currently easier than explaining all my ways of being and social nuances, and I am not sorry for being autistic. I am proud of who I am and my autism. I do not see it as "different but not less" as many others do. I see it as a completely valid way of being. It is a norm.

I don't actually want friends who judge me or are uncomfortable with me, or who don't love who I am. I now know that I am great and friendly, lovable, smart, funny, verbose, oversharing, and gorgeous.

It is OK to let someone know you find them attractive or like them, even if they aren't interested in you. You won't suffer any consequences.

Fear of rejection is so hard, especially when you're autistic, ADHD, and have RSD (rejection sensitivity dysphoria). But not understanding myself and these parts of me made everything so much harder growing up. I was terrified that people would find out I liked them and reject me. So I hung around groups of people, silently trying to fit in but never really knowing how to be myself. If I liked you, I just followed along with you, appeared to like the same things and hoped you would make all the decisions. But I wasted so much time on things I just didn't really like and not exploring things I did like. I wish I'd had the confidence growing up to just tell people something I liked about them and ask them about it. As an adult I can definitely tell that people enjoy talking about things they like. They love it when people ask them about their interests.

I now also give unsolicited compliments. If I see something I like, I tell that person, often a stranger, that I love the thing they are wearing, carrying, reading, listening to, etc. And I tell my friends things I love about them. If I notice a strength in them, I enjoy telling them. It is not forced, though. I only give genuine positive feedback. For example, I have told a friend that I love the way we can info-dump with each other concurrently without feeling pressured about being judged or upsetting each other with too much information. And that we can carry on two separate conversations simultaneously, where sharing encourages us equally. Another example is appreciating authenticity in a friend, who will tell you directly when you make them feel overwhelmed and will be honest about how they need to be supported or not. Or it could be telling someone you like their style. It doesn't have to be deep all the time. Compliments show you care and notice people in a positive way.

Not everyone else is being honest about everything

In general, I am genuine and since I like myself I don't see any reason to hide anything or pretend to be anyone else. I am blunt and direct in communication and I love it when others are too. I am not mean and I am not inferring more than I say. The expectation from others that there is additional meaning beyond the literal words I communicate can cause tensions that I often do not understand. When I don't understand, I ask questions. I try not to make assumptions about others. I find that not everyone else does this. Throughout my life I have come up against the inferences of others as a barrier to communication. I have found that people can take offence to my blunt and direct communication style and think I am being offensive when I have no intention of being so. This gets very confusing. And I find people often do not believe me when I am literally telling them what I mean. But not everyone is going to be open to honest and transparent communication. It does seem to be far worse within institutions (education, health, social services, etc.). I now know that when communicating with institutions, autistic people benefit greatly from having an advocate. Someone to back them up when they are communicating directly and honestly or to ask questions of institutions on their behalf in order to facilitate autistic needs being heard and seen as valid. I have also worked as an advocate for other autistic people. The system analytics part of my brain loves this work as I see the issues as communication systems and can identify where cogs are needing repair. And I can then use my words in the moment to add context or ask a question that prompts those involved to consider other perspectives. But as much as I am a great advocate for others, I still need to use advocates for myself too.

Spending money on yourself is not wasting money

Until my autism diagnosis at the age of 42 I really didn't understand myself. And I undervalued myself. I always felt less than worthy. This affected much in my life, from not contributing my own ideas to never buying nice clothes for myself. I didn't value myself. I was frustrated with myself. I have always enjoyed hand-me-down and second-hand clothes, shoes, and accessories. I love the stories things carry and embrace all that material culture studies have to offer in terms of the narratives of objects. But I felt guilty if I spent money on myself. I felt that I was wasting everyone's time in the whole world if I did something just for my own enjoyment. That's a seriously unnecessarily huge amount of pressure to place on myself! Especially as no one would even notice. But that didn't matter.

Through a creative art practice, I have found ways of exploring ideas, processing experiences and feelings, and exploring my own values. It also creates time and space for me to just be. It feels productive rather than self-indulgent, while fulfilling self-care needs. And I get a great sense of capability from creating things and a way of sharing and communicating with others. I work multimodally and don't resist what I work with. I incorporate my needs into how I work and give attention to what emerges inside my body as I create. I use creative expression to connect my logic-driven brain to my body and somatic experiencing. My sensory sensitivities are an incredible asset when working this way. I also use this insight and my wealth of experience to companion others in using the creative arts as a form of psychotherapy, with or without words. Through this I have created a career as a neurodivergent affirming creative arts therapist.

Not everyone will like you. Just like you don't actually like everyone else.

I grew up thinking it was important to be liked. To look for the good in others and be open-minded. I still see openness as a positive value. However, I know as an adult that having a couple of good friends makes for a wonderful life full of companionship. Having a huge friendship circle is not what matters. Finding people who love you for being you is so much more valuable than being likeable. And I don't actually like everyone else. I don't want fake friends. I want to be accepted, understood, valued, supported, challenged, and excited by my friendships. I am proud of and thankful for my friends. I still find it confusing when friendships change. All people change their priorities, interests, and values over time. It can be exhausting to maintain friendships that no longer grow with you and share your life. I am learning to let go, knowing that you can reconnect at any time when you align again.

There is no innate, right way to be

People make different choices when presented with the same logical information. Logic does not determine values, feelings, or correctness. And this is incredibly frustrating. Opinions are said to be like a*#holes – everyone has one. But as a deep thinker, I form my opinions based on evidence and research. If you utilize quality research, these then become informed opinions. And those I value and respect. When you clash with someone based on informed opinions, I find it an opportunity to engage in great discussion. This is without the aim of convincing one another, but to interrogate the available evidence and perspectives in order to feel fully informed.

The same goes with all elements of life. There is no one right way to live. It is great to know your options so you can make informed decisions. But how you choose to express who you are is valid. Life sometimes feels like it would be easier if there was a rule book and a formula, and if we all followed the same rules the outcomes would be predictable. But life is not like a video game. Life is not a competition and there is no timeline for achievements.

10
Ainslee Hooper

I'm Ainslee, and I'm a proud disabled person. It's taken me a long time to say those words. From Geelong, I live with my partner and our fur baby Sheldon (and yes, he is very much like his namesake, Sheldon Cooper, from *The Big Bang Theory*).

Growing up with a disability, I never thought I'd be living the life I have now. While growing up, it was like my life was set out for me, as if being born disabled instantly meant I had limited life choices and had to follow a particular path. I didn't know I had the option to live a life other than the one I was living. Therefore I didn't come to understand until much later that I was put on this earth to help people see the world through other people's eyes, to ensure everyone is heard, seen, and included. An Applied Anthropologist and Founder of Ainslee Hooper Consulting, my business is dedicated to helping remove invisible barriers and reduce the risk of ableism in medium- to large-sized public-facing businesses and organizations. Having previously worked in the public sector for 20 years, I never believed the saying, "Do a job you love, and you'll never work a day in your life" until I started my consultancy.

Even as recently as 2018, when I stepped out of the office for the last time, you would not recognize me as the same person I am today. Although I am an introvert and most consider me quiet, my ex-colleagues, who have attended some of my speaking engagements, are astounded at the confident and talkative person they see today. After an anthropology conference dinner, even my partner commented that what I said that night was the most he'd ever heard me speak. A stark difference to the person who would go to work every day with barely a peep, aside from answering customer enquiries!

In 2023, people with disabilities are still 40 years behind the women's equality movement. However, I look forward to a future where this gap no longer exists and disability inclusion is the norm. It's a slow process, with so many inspiring disability activists fighting for our rights since before I was even born. Still, it is a fight we must continue to ensure future generations don't have to.

If you'd like to join me in the fight to address the issues which perpetuate ableism and hinder inclusion, you can connect with me on LinkedIn (www.linkedin.com/in/ainsleehooper) or email me: info@ainsleehooper.com.au.

Ainslee's story – From you to me and me to you

Dear fifteen-year-old me,

I can't believe there are three whole decades between us; it feels like only yesterday. There is so much I want you to know about your life between then and now. I know it doesn't feel like it right now, but things DO get better. It probably sounds so cliché to you now, but it's true. As you already know, as a disabled teen life isn't always easy, and well, it's not always going to be a smooth ride along the way to 2023, but the journey will be worth it. In this letter, I will share some insights you need to know and give you some advice I wish had been given to me when I was you. Unfortunately, I can't change the experiences you're going to have. If I did, I wouldn't be able to write this letter to you now, nor would you be reading it (the rules of time travel). Still, I hope this letter from me to you will make the road from you to me a little less bumpy and more bearable.

As a fifteen-year-old disabled teenager, you're struggling with bullying at school. Many well-intentioned teachers will tell you you're being bullied because "people are afraid of what's different to them". This advice was not helpful; it just reinforced the idea that you're different. I mean, you are, but not in the way you were taught you were. You're different because you're you. There's only one of you; well, except for me. After having experienced bullying as an adult, I can honestly tell you it's not about you being disabled at all; it's about them. Unfortunately, you're just an easy target for them to take their unresolved issues out on.

You'll be told repeatedly that you need to fit in. Throughout your life, this idea will be fed to you in obvious and covert ways. You're already on your way to believing it. You've been told you're being bullied because you're different, and you'll be best suited for a job as a receptionist or secretary rather than being asked what you'd like to do. You believe these are your only options because you're not intelligent enough to be anything else. Not true. It's because you're a wheelchair user (yes, I don't say "person in a wheelchair" any more). The job options were limited because it was society's stock standard solution to disability employment in the 1990s. While things have gotten better 30 years later, the notion still exists. When you are in work, it's easier to fit you into a box than people thinking outside of it to give you the same opportunities as your peers. You'll also assume that you'll live with family for the rest of your life. I've got good news for you, though! You're now an anthropologist advising on disability inclusion, with two university degrees, a business owner, a published author, and an advisor on various committees and boards. You're also a homeowner living with your partner of 17 years and a fur baby.

Oh, by the way, remember when you were a kid, you used to spend hours organizing your coloured pencils and sequins only to pour them back into a pile and do it again? Or you'd spend hours colouring in the individual squares of graph paper? Or how much you enjoyed spending that six weeks' holiday break in the school library to help digitize the card catalogue? Yeah, you're autistic. It'll take 30 years to be diagnosed, for a couple of reasons. The first one is that the areas you've struggled with, like maths, learning to tie your shoelaces, and telling the time on an analogue clock have been attributed to your physical disability. Secondly, you're a girl; back then, girls went undiagnosed. Time travel and anthropology will become just a couple of your many special interests.

By the age of 15, you're already no stranger to hospitals. You've spent the first school term in hospital with doctors trying to figure out why you suffer chronic headaches. They never find a reason and will gaslight you into believing it's psychological. When you get your autism diagnosis, you'll find out that headaches are common in autistic people. By the time you're me, you'll have lost count of how many times you've been hospitalized for various reasons. You will have become accustomed to doctors making assumptions about you and your treatment because of your disability. You'll come to believe you're a burden because of overt and covert messaging. But luckily, by the time you're me, you'll come to unlearn this idea and understand the internalized ableism (a word used to describe disability discrimination) you've leaned into to rationalize the negative experiences due to being disabled.

Speaking of internalized ableism, I know you're reading this screwing up your face at the idea of working on anything related to disability and wondering how on earth you'd end up working in a part of your identity you'd shun if you could. Due to all of your experiences, even at the age of 15, you've been taught to be ashamed of your disability. It's something that's being used against you to hold you back, to make you feel like you're inadequate. You also resent anyone telling you that you'd be perfect for a job related to disability because, like the recommended secretary and receptionist roles, this unsolicited advice is based on nothing but assumptions about you. It wasn't something that was ever planned. Still, as a result of the experiences you've had, combined with those you're yet to have as a disabled person, you'll come to realize that your degree in anthropology (which you only pursued because of the few individuals who believed in you) is the perfect way to address the many issues in society you've become aware of while being disabled.

This is the part of the letter where I want to give you some advice that I wish someone had given me when I was your age. Firstly, never be ashamed of who you are. Hopefully, it's already evident to you, but I'll repeat it so it sinks in. The shame you feel now about being disabled is not because there is something wrong with you, it's because of how society thinks about disability – and you've taken on those messages as a coping mechanism. Be proud of being unique, quirky, awkward, nerdy, and all the other things that make up you and me, individual that you are. Embrace your disability, as it's as much a part of you as the freckles on your skin and your wild red hair.

My second piece of advice is not to be afraid to use your voice and advocate for yourself. You'll be taught to accept the status quo, but that doesn't mean you have to. It's your life, and you have dreams and aspirations like everyone else. They're just unrealized because no one has bothered to ask you what you want. That's why taking up space is important; I want you to know it's OK to do so. It will take practice but it will be worth it. Like my favourite disability advocate and poet Laura Hershey says, "you get proud by practising". If you can, check out her poems, they're words I wish I had come across when I was your age.

My final piece of advice to you is this: Never apologize or thank anyone for being included. Being disabled is not a valid reason for you to be excluded from something. You'll think it's normal to thank someone when you encounter inclusion, but that's because it's so uncommon for you. Likewise, you'll feel the urge to apologize when requesting accommodations for your access needs to be met. Don't! It's your human right to expect access to the same places, spaces, and opportunities as your peers. You're not expecting too much to have your human rights met.

If I had to write all of this as a message in a bottle, I'd tell you to be proud of who you are. You are NOT a burden; you are strong, intelligent, and precisely who you are meant to be.

I'll see you when you get here!

11
Jack Brady

Jack Brady (they/them) is an occasional variety artist, independent producer, and anthropologist/political scientist. They are a proudly ace nonbinary transmasculine autistic human, with a passion for morbid history, acronyms, alliterations, and inappropriate musical comedy composition. They are currently completing a PhD in political science on the politics of laughter in the Australian political comedy scene.

Jack's story

Dear Jack,

I'm here, looking back at you. I'm holding space for you, some 36 years later. I know I can't change anything. I wish I could tell you just how much this journey called life will bring you back to you, back from what society thinks you should be. Your story is a story for young people now, about hope and following your passions. But it's also a story about the power of a child's first champion. So, your story is also a story of hope for the parents of children who don't fit the mould too.

Sixteen. Molly Ringwald and popular culture abounds with messages about girls, sweetness, and light. Forgiving. Yielding. Feminine.

You're none of those things. None of those things make sense to you. You can shoot a gun, stitch up an injured horse, groom other people's horses for a gymkhana so you can pay the bills for your own horse. The people that come to you have money like your family will never have. You talk too much and about things no one else is interested in and then you shut down for long periods of silence.

There are times when you will experience going inside yourself in such a way that the rest of the people around you will take you to doctors and tag you with the wrong labels. But I need you to know, that's okay. It's more than okay. It's who you are, autistic, and the world will wake up in time.

You like to work alone and to be taught one on one by someone who explains things properly. Your dad is master of the patient-step-by-step.

Then you like to be left alone to try yourself, coming back only when you need help. Your dad also lets you do this, he does not hover, he does not correct, he stands back (unless you are unsafe). Right now, I have to tell you just how much you will be like him. In your fifties you'll teach at university, and you'll be the kind of facilitator of knowledge who lets people grow, and when you do your heart will fill with an energy that will drive you on when most give up.

It's that energy that comes through the parts of you that come from your dad, and your expression of your deep interest in the world around you. Don't let that go, not ever.

That passion you have for things that interest you – it is a skill. It's not just a skill, it's the skill.

As I close my eyes, I can take my mind back to look through your eyes to one of those moments in time and I see you as you lay on the grass. You look up at Chasta's Appaloosa underbelly as she calmly grazes, the crickets creating their own frequency in the Wooroi forest air. It's the kind of frequency that stills your mind, unlike the other cacophonies at home. The TV, the awful fluorescent lights, people talking next door, car doors slamming. "But it's a quiet area", everyone says.

Where you keep Chasta, in a paddock on loan on the edge of a state forest in a small coastal town, is a housing estate now. But in the 1980s, Chasta's paddock was a clearing among a network of sandy busy tracks and dense semi-tropical forest.

The owner of this paddock is a local "eccentric" who lives away from everyone in a strange house in the back of the forest, like some woodsman from a fairy tale. He happens to like your dad and he doesn't seem to like many people. He lets you and your dad keep the agistment here for free so Chasta can graze. Well, not for free, but in exchange for keeping the fences okay and keeping other people out.

You love disappearing out with the horses and fixing a fence with Dad. Working silently and collaboratively together, as father and Jack did. A safe zone, in that quiet forest paddock, tightening wires, not saying much and just enjoying doing things together.

He is also giving you something precious here, and that's about future work. Everyone in your house does not go to work. Your dad was medically retired at 48, just a year after your birth. He was 20 years older than your mum. He must keep his physical efforts to a minimum and your mum has a range of mental health conditions that won't be fully appreciated until her seventies. No one comes home at the end of the day and tells you what work was like.

So your fence fixing and tool shed time with your father will become the basis of your understanding of the world of work. You will expect everyone to be patient and kind and although your working life will be challenging you will stand fast in trying to stay patient and kind – and I want to tell you to be proud of that.

But when you start working, following a family tradition of military service, it's going to be a massive shock. But you will get through. You will also, I am proud to say, realize that this family tradition needs to be broken and step away from old ideas about service and even teach critiques of militarization at university in the future.

The interests sparked in your brain by your rerunning of *The Sound of Music* over and over will serve you well. You couldn't get enough of the Von Trapp family and the reasons they fled. Why do people do these things to each other? Why? It will fuel your later life, working on issues of social justice and positive change.

You will forever do a dance with your mum back and forth; from love to bitterness, hope to disappointment. There will be a moment at the end of her life where it appears like you finally understand each other. It is what it is. You need to just know that as a child you have no influence over this; that she is her own person. You are not an extension of her.

The forest is more than an escape. Out here in the forest and surrounded by nature will always be your go-to place. The sound of the TV that is almost constantly on at home and makes you want to scream fades as you ride away towards the bush track.

Chasta (and the dogs that will follow her) is the only being that seems to get you. She's afraid of wombats and puddles and you're afraid of most people. But unlike your horse you don't show your fear; you do your best to mimic others around you, anything to fit in. You internalize that fear. In your late thirties you'll learn you don't need to do that anymore.

That day in the forest, the one that springs to my memory today, the wildflowers were blooming. It had been unseasonal weather and colder than usual. You wove them into a necklace and put them around Chasta's neck. She then ate them. Late bloomer. Yep, that will be you. It will take you a long time to figure out that you really don't need to get married and have children. But you will mimic again, and things will get tough. But you are strong, you are resilient. You will not keep pursuing these things in your forties and you'll settle into a happy state of queerness.

I remember that day you escaped to the forest with Chasta because you broke Dad's VCR player. One too many plays of *The Sound of Music* and smoke poured out of it.

You lay out there in that little clearing surrounded by soothing cricket noise for hours with Chasta. Dad was so proud of that VCR; we were the first people in the street to have one. He wasn't mad, but it was Mum whose wrath you feared. But it wasn't like a yelling wrath. It was a seething critical wrath filled full of expressions that made no sense. A nice tone with a nasty message that you could never work out. And then she would get angry at you because you did not know how to respond.

The tone was lost on you. What you will later learn through your studies is that this is called passive aggression, and to your literal consciousness of course it didn't make sense. And when you couldn't understand why the sweet tone didn't match the horrible message, she called you names. She said you had no common sense. But Dad, Dad said you were smart.

And here I am now, looking through your eyes at Chasta and the wildflowers, telling you just how smart you are.

You may not believe it now, and I'm sure others around you now wouldn't either, but there is a really interesting future ahead of you. You'll focus on your dad's words. You'll listen to stories of his life, of repairing remote lighthouses all around Australia. Of the Min Min lights in remote Queensland. Of doing seismic line mapping throughout the Northern Territory.

You'll listen and absorb this message and that mimic in you will move from mimic to creator of your own path. Your own life will be filled with anthropological journeys and culture and nature. Somewhere in your heart you'll find that this is the message you have no choice but to follow – to go with your passions is like the crickets' urge to rub their legs together.

You'll take on a profession to learn more about the secret language of other people around you and you'll be good at it. You'll joke on a comedy stage one day in your forties that "I help people solve problems they didn't know they had".

Dad always took you away from Mum and would argue you needed skills. But it was really so you could hang out with him and hide. In the tool shed. Making things, fixing cars with the most patient human around you. All the stuff that got you a similar reaction from the girls at school to the one you got from Mum. The tut-tut-tutting. The accusations you are there to find a husband.

The thing I know now is, in 2023, being able to pull apart a car engine or use a bandsaw when you are someone assigned female at birth (AFAB) is a skill that many still don't have. I wish I could tap you on the shoulder and say you'll be able to split rim and patch whole 4WD tyres in remote Australian locations. You'll create maps and use GPS and walk alongside Aboriginal people as they map sacred sites. You'll travel the world, notably not to cities much, but to places of great beauty and history. You will continue all the childhood "boy" things you did with Dad, and they'll be assets. Even in your fifties.

And eventually, you'll step out of the gender binary and you won't care at all what others think of that. Be proud of that. Wear it with pride. You didn't have to conform to gender stereotypes; no one has to. You'll play the traditional feminine game from time to time. But you'll always revert to your gender-fluid happy place.

Oh, I am sure some of those girls at school who teased you would now regret saying those things. And your mum, she will eventually embrace who you really are. But if I could come back and tell you one thing to change, it would be that hope is for your heart, not for your mother's. You don't need to hope for her to "have a change of heart". Let your own heart beat for yourself first. Her hopes for you are her own, not yours.

You will never go to a high school reunion because you will never be asked to one. And you won't be bothered in the slightest. You suspect you didn't get asked because you didn't finish year

12; you only got to the end of year 11 and left. But you can't help but think that there is likely a forgetting of you in this non-invitation too.

Someone you know will go. They will report back to you that they told them about your career in anthropology, your travels, your comedy. And one of those mean girls will gasp and say "I knew it, I knew they would do something incredible".

Oh, what delicious irony. The taunts about you only doing technical things for the boys' attention, when it was the last thing on your mind.

Oh! If only they knew how you gazed at that tall slender girl with the sweet round lips. How you knew that boys were what you were meant to covet, but that you only played the game of a carrot on a stick. You only decided to try and get married to a man and have babies because that was all you thought there was. You thought you were an anomaly, that there was something wrong with your feelings.

What you also learn from Dad is to walk alongside people – don't judge, just be there. You'll be good at this, because you don't really want to know why someone's appearance is supposed to be important.

In my mind's eye I can hear the crickets in the forest, as you lie on the grass looking up at the sky watching the clouds. It's getting late. Chasta is snoozing on her feet, a happy horse. You'll love her so very much.

You'll daydream of lighthouses. You'll picture yourself as Indiana Jones with a sense of ethics and without the awful grave robbing, because that part of those movies makes you really mad and sparks debate at home.

One day, in your fifties, your adult offspring will chuckle in reflection, and you'll ask them why. They will reply "you don't have fancy things around you, you have things that mean stuff. You have rocks you were given by a Traditional Owner. You have feathers and camel bags. It's the little things that tell a big story. You are who you wanted to be as a kid, that's pretty cool".

You'll end up in this place of men's suits, corduroy pants, short hair with splashes of colour, and mixed-up palettes of plaids and checks. In this place of a never-ending supply of philosophy texts that bring you more joy than any Netflix episode ever can.

If I could warn you, I would. It's going to get hard, only to get much better. There'll be illness (yours and others') and death. You'll have to learn to argue and debate like an academic (which you will become) and map and change tyres and listen hard to the world. You'll have to manage the sensory world you live in, often by disappearing to remote or regional places, and that's okay. You may never reach the same financial goals as others of your age because you will need more time off in exchange for that full life. What most find easy you will find hard, and what most find hard you will find easy.

You'll also witness some of the worst and some of the best of humanity, up close. You will lose your beloved father way too early, but you will never lose his champion's heart. It beats in yours.

Let the memory of your childhood champion never dwindle. Let that be your compass for living.

It's all worth it. Don't let anyone tell you any different.

Right now, I want to look through your eyes and tell you, go well. Go well and when you come across others like you, tell them to follow their passions.

You are going to break open family patterns and build your own lineage of freedom and that is your neurodivergent gift to yourself first, the world second.

Love

Jack

12
Kat Reed

Kat (they/them/theirs) has been a local queer and disability advocate and community builder in the ACT (Australian Capital Territory) for the last ten years. They are currently the CEO of Women with Disabilities ACT and a Board Director of Women with Disabilities Australia and of Youth Coalition of the ACT. Kat was recently awarded 2021 Young Canberra Citizen of the Year and one of Out for Australia's 30 Under 30 for 2021.

Their activism and community building work spans many different intersections. Since the age of 17, they have advocated for the rights of people of colour, queer youth, trans and non-binary people, and people with disabilities.

They've held positions of leadership in both local and national organizations, including the ANU Students' Association, and led the Australian Queer Students' Network as the National Co-Convenor.

Kat is also a political performance artist and through their arts persona they recently finished work on Australia's very first all-trans and gender-diverse original musical titled *Lost in Transit*, with a cast of six local trans and gender diverse artists.

Kat's alternative persona is as a burlesque and drag artist, DJ, and cabaret vocalist – exploring political themes through a queer reading of sci-fi.

When Kat isn't busy advocating, they're either curling up at home with their pet lizard or drinking something from their enormous tea collection.

Kat's story

Dear 16-year-old me,

As I gather the various aspects of myself around a metaphorical roundtable, I am filled with a sense of awe and wonder. Here we are, the fragments of our existence converging to reflect upon the woven tapestry of our lived experiences. In this letter to you, I invite each part of myself that is the now 27-year-old to share their wisdom, offering some guidance on the path we have traversed and the path that you are about to trek.

At the head of the table you sit, Sixteen, who has only just stepped into the world, embracing their newfound identity with a sense of peace. Little did they know that this journey of self-discovery and acceptance was only the beginning. Sixteen, your queerness will become the catalyst for a career in advocacy, a path that will shape your purpose and impact the lives of many.

Seventeen emerges, bursting out of their bubble and embarking on a project to promote LGBTQIA+ inclusion. In doing so, they grapple with uncertainties and fears, questioning whether they have made a mistake by exposing themselves to a potentially harsh world. But they push through, driven by a desire to understand themselves and create a more inclusive environment. Seventeen's honesty and boldness will bring new friends into their life. **Chosen family.**

Moving around the table, we meet Eighteen, brimming with confidence and enthusiasm for life. They experience the exhilarating rush of first love, but also encounter heartbreak and abuse. The pain leaves lasting scars, both physical and emotional. It has been said that when it comes to trauma, the body holds the memories. And theirs will remember for far longer than you thought possible. They'll struggle through a fog of dissonant memories, remembering the good times, which make the bad times seem unreal.

Yet Eighteen finds solace in education, exploring queer theory, gender studies, and feminism and entering into the new social silo of university. These newfound perspectives reshape their view of the world and themselves.

Nineteen, weary from leading a queer community group and navigating a painful breakup, confronts depression for the first time. The experience is terrifying. Mounting stress begins to take its toll, raising questions about their well-being. That phantom pain in their left leg, the 4 p.m. bedtimes… Something was not right.

Twenty arrives, looking at bathrooms through a different lens, and questioning the conventional binary options. Male or female? Neither was the answer. A wise friend said that everyone should question their gender at some point in their lifetime. This is when you questioned yours and found a euphoric feeling every time someone used your new pronouns. You'll never go back to using she/her pronouns again. Yet, despite this revelation, Twenty still faces ongoing challenges, grappling with fatigue, social difficulties, and mysterious memory lapses. Remembering the details of Eighteen's relationship seems so difficult to Twenty now. Maybe it didn't really happen? **Perhaps they were the toxic one?**

Twenty-one, now firmly grounded in their racial identity, confronts insecurities stemming from societal expectations and biases. Being an adult and surrounded by all sorts of people with an assortment of backgrounds and ethnicities will force Twenty-one to confront something they've always deep-down thought about themselves – they believed they were ugly. The times they were teased for having "strange food" (the food was often much better in quality), or the times when they overheard their peers declare "Asians" couldn't be beautiful. Even the time they themselves teased a fellow student, all because they weren't comfortable with themselves. Twenty-one realized their multiracial features are beautiful just as they are – no one looks like them.

Additionally, Twenty-one embraces their identity as a person on the asexual spectrum, finding solace in the fluidity of their sexuality. Grey-asexual, it seems you are destined to forever be in the middle of all spectrums.

Twenty-two stumbles upon a word that encapsulates their struggles – an acknowledgement of their need for accommodations and support in their daily life. **Disability.** This realization marks the beginning of their journey towards understanding and identifying with their disabilities, encompassing trauma, depression, anxiety, and an unnamed internal struggle.

Twenty-three completes their university education and enters the workforce, leaving behind the perpetual cycle of stress and burnout. This year becomes a period of recovery and reflection, paving the way for decisions about the future.

Twenty-four witnesses dreams becoming reality, as they ascend to the position of CEO of an advocacy organization at a young age. **You did it! This is what Sixteen dreamt of!**

Twenty-five blazes forward, facing the most challenging year in their professional life yet. But Twenty-five thrives in the deep, and despite stress and burnout threatening to topple them, Twenty-five will make it through.

Moreover, as the journey unfolds, an experience that lay dormant for almost a decade resurfaces, compelling Twenty-five to summon their courage, resilience, and insight. They must now delve into the depths of their inner psyche, bravely facing the haunting shadows of abuse and trauma that have plagued them since their tender days of Nineteen. The road that lies ahead for Twenty-five is strewn with obstacles and challenges, but Twenty-five has Twenty-six and Twenty-seven as friends along the journey.

To all other fragments at the table, learn from Twenty-five's example. You are the architect of your own resilience, and with every step forward you pave the way to a life imbued with strength, authenticity, and boundless possibility.

A revelation reshapes the world of Twenty-six – ADHD. The diagnosis brings a mix of grief and sadness – life could have been so different with earlier recognition! After years of seeing counsellors, doctors, of feeling depressed and of struggling with their memory, energy, and productivity… this is why. **You are neurodivergent. Your brain works differently!** As the years unfold, Twenty-six, alongside others who will join the table, will embrace their neurodivergence as an integral part of their identity. They will explore strategies, tools, and resources that enable them to harness their strengths and navigate the challenges that come with their unique wiring. And one day soon, perhaps Twenty-six will receive a letter from their future self.

Returning to you, Sixteen, at the head of the table, I see you treading water in an ocean of emotions. Each wave carries conflicting currents of euphoria, anxiety, uncertainty, and vulnerability. Amidst this tumult, you navigate with resilience, aware that within the depths of your emotions lies the potential for profound self-discovery and growth.

You have only just begun to explore the vastness of the world. You have found peace in embracing your queerness, but the journey ahead is filled with transformative experiences that will shape you in unimaginable ways. Embrace the overwhelming emotions, for they are the catalysts of growth.

As you embark on the path that lies ahead, remember the lessons and wisdom offered by each fragment of our existence. Cherish the resilience, the self-acceptance, and the advocacy that have blossomed within you. May the years to come be filled with growth, discovery, and a deep sense of fulfilment.

I'm only 27 now, so here's to many more letters to come…

Warmest regards,

Kat

13
Margherita Coppolino

Margherita is a lesbian with disability from a culturally and linguistically diverse (CALD) background. She brings expertise from her intersectional lived experience as well as her activism, advocacy, and professional experience. Margherita has been representing and working on issues for women, people with disability, CALD and disability communities since 1980.

Margherita has extensive knowledge and experience working with LGBTQIA+ communities and allies. She is well known and well regarded across LGBTQIA+ communities in Victoria, Australia, Oceania and beyond, particularly for her advocacy around LGBTQIA+ disability intersectionality. She is considered as a lesbian elder within Victorian LGBTQIA+ communities.

Margherita currently holds positions as Co-Chairperson of ILGA Oceania and board member of ILGA World. She has been appointed to the Victorian Government LGBTIQA+ Taskforce. She is Deputy President of Drummond Street Services' board and a founding member and Secretary on the management committee of Inclusive Rainbow Voices (LGBTIQA+ People with Disability).

Margherita's story – The little book of life

Introduction

My name is Margherita Coppolino. I was born on 6 August 1960 at the Royal Women's Hospital in Melbourne. I spent the first 17 years of my life in institutional care, not knowing and having no contact with my parents or my extended family. Effectively I was an orphan. I am also a first-generation migrant and I have dwarfism. I am now 60 years old. This collection of characteristics has in many ways shaped my life. I wonder how my life would be if my mother as an 18-year-old had not given me up for adoption? This question and others relating to my identity will shape the life story that I am writing.

Early days

Let's go back to the beginning. My mother Rosa came from a Sicilian village called Castroreale. In 1959, when she was 18, she migrated, on her own, to Australia. She was planning to join her father who had come out to Australia just after the end of the Second World War. Her father was living in Maidstone (an inner western and working-class suburb of Melbourne). The two of them were going to earn enough money to bring the rest of the Coppolino family out to Australia.

When the boat arrived at Melbourne, Rosa was pregnant. Later I was told that her pregnancy was the result of a rape while on the ship. For a time, Rosa worked as a machinist in Flinders Lane, which was then the centre of the "rag trade".

In the last few weeks of her pregnancy Rosa was at St Joseph's Home in Broadmeadows. When I was born she named me Margherita and signed adoption papers. She was told that I couldn't be adopted because of my dwarfism. I spent two and a half years at St Joseph's. Initially my mother had to pay a maintenance fee, but eventually I was made a ward.

I was then transferred to St Catherine's. Later, when I was 12, I was sent to the St Vincent de Paul Homes in Black Rock.

Life in institutional care

I have no memory of my time at St Joseph's. There is, however, a story about me. This was told to me later by Sr Genevieve, a much-loved nun at St Catherine's. The story goes that as toddlers we were all in our cots. I climbed out, let the sides down of all the other cots then opened the door. The other children got out of their cots and wandered out of the room. Meanwhile I climbed back into my cot and behaved as if nothing had happened!

I moved to St Catherine's when I was about three. St Catherine's was a large old convent set in 42 acres of land. There was a separate house for the priest on site. I think there were about 200 children in my time, all girls, as the boys, once they turned five, were sent to St Augustine's. It is almost inconceivable now that children could be brought up in this institutional environment. Life at St Catherine's was almost completely self-contained. All of the services were on-site. We ate in the dining room, the "mess", we played outside together (there was a sand pit and later a pool), there were chooks [chickens], we went to the internal school on the ground floor together, and we slept in dormitories. We went to mass on Sundays. This was our world.

I was a "tomboy". I climbed trees and I played football. I don't recall having any special friends, but I was easy to get on with without being close to anyone. I remember going to some holiday hosts (holiday hosts were "good" people who, every holiday, would take a child from the orphanage and be "kind" to them) and coming back with a bag of lollies. These were taken away from me and put into a high cupboard in the kitchen. Then a bath upstairs started to overflow and the water started pouring out. The nuns went upstairs to sort it out, leaving us unsupervised in the "mess". I went into the kitchen, pulled out the drawers underneath the bank of cupboards and used the drawers as steps. Then I reached up, opened the cupboard door and retrieved my lollies. I then shared them with the other children.

When I was at St Catherine's it was obvious that I looked physically different to the other girls. I was of short stature. This was just how it was. I was one of the girls. I felt included in activities and not at all discriminated against. Sr Genevieve played a part in this. I remember on sports day (I was not a great athlete!) Sr Genevieve asked me to be the signpost for the events. The other girls had to run around me, the signpost. I gave them directions.

When I got older I started to have regular sessions at the Royal Children's Hospital. I realized I was different when I became part of a research programme into short-statured persons. Although I enjoyed learning I had a genetic hearing problem and dyslexia. I remember being at the Children's Hospital when I was made to stand in front of a group of young doctors in my underclothes. And they were there to see me about my hearing!

I think the "welfare" wanted to help me. But it didn't feel right. One day a short-statured couple came to see me at the home.

I think the idea was that it would make me comfortable about my "disability". It felt odd. I spent many holidays with a holiday host couple at Swan Hill and I quite enjoyed spending time with them. Other children came too. Three of these children were then adopted by the couple. I wasn't. This hurt me very much.

I asked: "Why don't you want me?" I was told I was different, that it wouldn't be suitable and that there were better opportunities for me in Melbourne. I asked Sr Genevieve. She told me: "Yes, you are different. God made you different. You are special."

I left St Catherine's when I was 12 and moved to Melbourne. I spent the next six years of my life in St Vincent de Paul homes, starting in a hostel of about ten girls that was behind the convent in Black Rock. For the first time in my life, I went, in sixth grade, to an "outside" school.

It took a lot of adjusting. After 12 months in the hostel, I was moved to the new model of "out of home care", the family group home. The family group home was an attempt to replicate a "family environment". The carers were a live-in couple and there were fewer children. I lived in a family group home in Caulfield and, from memory, there were about seven children. The carers came and went. I remember there being two sets of parents. One set of carers had two small children.

I found that whole period of my life challenging. We were in adolescence and facing the turmoil of emotions and feelings that time of life brings. I struggled at secondary school, the O'Neill Girls College (later taken over by Star of the Sea). My file describes me as "not coping" and "not settling". I went to counselling at the Royal Children's Hospital in the Short Stature Clinic. I think most of my turmoil revolved around identity. Who am I? My relationships with my carers, the other children, and with my counsellor and the welfare's case worker(s) were superficial. I did not trust anyone enough to expose myself to emotional scrutiny. I don't think any of the adults who were involved with me ever understood or captured the inner child in me. To be fair, I am not sure I did either. This has been a search all my life.

At 17, I left the family group home and moved into a hostel with other older girls. This was to prepare us for life after school. Aunty Ollie was in charge. She was a wonderful person.

Discovering my family

I have made many efforts, over many, many years to find my family. It started after I left "care". I was in my twenties at the time and was able to get a copy of my "welfare" file. This helped me locate my grandfather (who of course was a Coppolino). He still lived in Maidstone. One day I simply arrived at their front gate. I wrote a note saying who I was and details of how I could be got in touch with and left it on the front door. I remember walking back to the gate as the front door opened. A man was in the doorway. He took one look at me and his shoulders slumped. He knew by my appearance who I was. He walked back inside and shut the door.

A couple of years later I went back again. This time I took a friend who spoke Italian. My friend knocked on the door and a boy answered it. She was told to come back later. We did. When we came back there was an old man watering the garden. This was my grandfather, Rosa's father. My friend and he spoke in Italian for a bit. What she told me he said to her was: "Leave us alone. This is another nail in the coffin."

So that was that.

I went to see a clairvoyant. What she did is unfathomable. She looked at me and she decided not to do a reading. She knew nothing about me. Instead, she gave me a phone number. It was the number of VANISH, which is a small not-for-profit organization which helps adults locate their family of origin. How did she know this would help me?

I rang VANISH and told them my story. Within two days they had located my mother. The staff had done a search at Births Deaths and Marriages (BDM). They located my birth certificate and looked for a marriage certificate for my mother, Rosa. They found it. My mother was married on 17 July 1962, just two years after I was born. Then they searched the electoral rolls, looking for Rosa under her married name, Veri. She lived at 4 McKenzie St Reservoir. I wrote to her, introducing myself and asking if I could meet her. There was no response.

In the early 1990s I appeared on the Derryn Hinch show, titled *Hinch*, as a Mother's Day story. This came about following an approach by *Hinch* to VANISH. VANISH recommended me as someone to interview about trying to track down their missing mother. I was interviewed by a journalist and the interview went on air. I said I wanted to meet my mother and that I was proud to be a Coppolino. The story got some publicity but there was no response from my family.

Three or four years later, with encouragement from my friends, I tried again. They pointed out to me that I had her address and her phone number. I think my mother always knew that I would contact her. I think she was waiting for it. We spoke on the phone and I told her that I had forgiven her for giving me up. We have not spoken since and I have never met her.

At about the same time I received more information from the "welfare". They told me that I had three half siblings: Linda, Angela, and Frank. Their father had died in the late 1990s.

In 2012 I contacted my brother Frank. He had no idea I existed or that I was born with dwarfism. He demanded that I prove my "identity". I gave him copies of my birth certificate and our mother's marriage certificate. I got the impression that he was keen to meet, but he said that he would talk about this with his sisters (they are my sisters too!). He got back to me and said: "Now is not the right time to meet. We'll get in touch with you sometime in the future."

I remember my brother Frank saying that he wished he had known about me. That is, he wished he'd known about my dwarfism before he had children. I don't deny my dwarfism. It's a part of my life that I embrace.

I believe that when my mother dies, and she is now in her eighties, I will be able to meet and talk with my siblings.

My siblings are now known to me and by the connectivity of social media I can, from a distance, follow their lives. I can be connected through common friends and mutual attendance at an Italian restaurant. At the moment I am content with this.

Adulthood: Employment

My first paid job was working in Prahran as a packer for a clothing manufacturer. All day I would fold and pack lingerie into bags ready for delivery. This was OK but I did think there was more to work than this. I knew I could do better.

I got some help from the Commonwealth Rehabilitation Service (CRS). CRS was a publicly funded organization (its functions have now all been privatized) that provided rehab, training, and placement services for many with disabilities. It assisted me to apply for a job with the Commonwealth public service. I was successful and was placed with the Australian Bureau of Statistics. I spent ten years there as a clerical assistant.

Greener fields attracted me. I applied for other positions and ended up in the Commonwealth Employment Service (then a division of the Department of Social Security) as a personnel officer. Inevitably there was a restructure and I moved across to Social Security, working as an employment officer. I spent three years there.

The State Labor governments of John Cain and Joan Kirner established a new programme, Job Link, in the Department of Labour. This involved working with the long-term unemployed. Many in this category had a variety of disabilities. I carried a caseload of about 30. Our task was job preparation and placement. The arrival of Jeff Kennett, in 1992, saw the programme and me (and many others!) made redundant. The experience in the state public service was my first exposure to systemic discrimination. I was of short stature and had sight and hearing difficulties. This meant that I was never allowed to gain permanency in the public service. Much of my life has been spent fighting against this systemic and overt type of discrimination.

At the time I was studying for a Diploma of Training and Education at Melbourne University. Some friends suggested I start my own business as a consultant working with disability and employment issues. I called it "Unlimited Growth". I did odds and ends of training and then picked up a 12-month contract with Australia Post. This was an impressive, forward-looking organization. My role was to develop a disability recruitment programme. I was made to feel part of the organization. New staff at Australia Post were expected to "be a postie for a day" to gain on-the-ground experience. This was going to be a problem for me. Australia Post, however, set me up in a sidecar attached to a motorbike and we followed the postie up and down streets.

Next followed eight months at Westpac, where I was asked to develop a Disability Action Plan. By this stage I had finished my diploma in training and education and had gone on to complete my degree. Looking back, and this is 25 years ago, these were major achievements. I was becoming an informed and sought-after consumer advocate and policy wonk for disability issues and I was mixing more in the corporate world. I served on the Board of the Diversity Council of Australia, which operated under the umbrella of the Business Council of Australia. In the late 1990s I was the inaugural winner of the Olive Zhakarov Award for my work at Australia Post.

Advocacy

In 2021, as part of Disability Awards, I was inducted into the Disability Lifetime Achievement Honour Roll.

This award has given me the opportunity to reflect on both my advocacy commitment and my advocacy practice.

I became very aware early in my life what a positive difference people could make to the lives of others. The example set by these people became the model for me. I made a commitment that I too would work with others to improve our collective circumstances. I have been very privileged to work alongside people who have made a similar commitment. It is fabulous to see what a difference can be made.

I want to see all intersectional communities working together for the common good. Covid has given us the opportunity to see the gaps that exist in our society. If we are able to step back and look after each other we will achieve more. I want to see fewer silos in both service provision and in public policy.

I was really flattered to be nominated for the award. It is an honour to be recognized for a lifetime's work and commitment. It is also an honour for and a wonderful reflection on all the people that I have worked with. All these people have collectively worked to improve the quality of individual lives and make the society we live in a better place. Together we can make a difference. Some of the things I have been involved in that have made a difference are:

I became the consumer representative for different federal government departments' reference groups and undertook advocacy work for Women with Disabilities, Australia.

For five years (2006–2011) I worked with the state government's Department of Planning and Community Development to create a Disability Action Plan. The Liberals returned to power in 2011 and my programme and I were again made redundant.

I have always done a lot of voluntary work. The line between my paid and unpaid work is blurry. It is always about the issue, not the reward.

Most recently I have been President of the National Ethnic Disability Alliance and served on the Boards of Drummond St and Footscray Community Arts Centre. I am currently a Director on ILGA World Board and Co-Chair of ILGA Oceania (ILGA – International, Lesbian, Gay, Transgender, and Intersex Association). Current member of the LGBTQIA+ Victorian Ministerial Task Force. In 2018 and 2021, I appeared at the United Nations CRPD COSP11 and COSP13 side event on the panel talking about LGBTQIA+ people with disabilities.

In 2021, I was inducted into the Victorian Disability Lifetime Achievements roll, and in 2022, I won Victoria LGBTIQ+ Person of the Year.

Activities and interests

But it's not all work! I have always had an interest in photography. Most recently I have had an exhibition at Federation Square called "The Golden Moment". This showcases a series of photos that I took at the World Dwarf Games.

In 2016, I was a collaborating artist in the "Silent Tears" exhibition, which revealed the lived experience of women with disability who are subjected to violence and women who acquired disability as a result of violence. The Silent Tears Project was showcased at the United Nations as part of the 60th session of the United Nations Commission on the Status of Women in New York, USA.

I have taken to sport and athletics later in life. There were no opportunities for people of small stature to compete when I was young. I represented Australia in 2009, 2013, and 2017 at the World Dwarf Games, held respectively in Ireland, the US, and

Canada. I had success in Bocce, winning Gold and Silver in 2013 and two Silver in 2017. I competed in power lifting in 2017 and won Gold, lifting 53 kg. And broke a world record in power lifting.

Discovering my culture

I went to Sicily in 2009, to the village of Castroreale. This was a village of about 2,500 people. It had 80 churches. Some of the houses dated back to the thirteenth century. The Coppolinos had lived here for generations.

I was so welcomed. I met the regulator of the village and he told me that I was always welcome in the village and that he and others would tell the Coppolino family that I am a part of this village. Then I went up to the top of a hill that stood behind the village and looked out. I could see the city of Messina spread out before me. It was wonderful and I felt empowered. I felt I belonged and that I had come back to my beginnings.

There was a story about me in the local newspaper.

Creating my identity

Who am I? This is the question I can remember asking the nuns who looked after me when I was a child. This curiosity is also noted in my child welfare file. I was not raised by my mother and I was not raised in my culture. I looked different to the other children in the orphanage, and I had strong feelings of attraction to same sex people that I did not understand. How have I become what I am today? My story is in many ways about how I put all these pieces of my life together.

Coming out

In 2005 I was asked by Tony, editor of the *SSPA* (Short Statured People of Australia) *Journal*, to write about coming out as a lesbian. This invitation allowed me to revisit the different experiences I had in coming out in different parts of my life such as friends, work, social groups, etc.

However, first let me take you on a journey of my coming to terms with my sexuality:

During my teens, I never had crushes on any boys but had a major crush on my sports teacher. I thought that there was something wrong with me, having been raised by Mercy nuns in the orphanage. You see, the Catholic Church didn't approve of homosexuality. With this belief haunting me, I struggled for all of my teens with my feelings and the crushes I had on females.

When I turned 18, I was no longer under the guardianship of the Victorian Government and the Mercy nuns. I moved into a flat of my own in St Kilda and adjusted to mainstream society, when I learned to improve my social skills, and gained employment and made friends. I was also very active in SSPA and doing lots of public speaking on short-statured issues.

Then International Day of Persons with Disabilities took place for the first time in 1981 on 3 December. During this era, Affirmative Action and Equal Opportunity legislation was being drafted. It was an exciting time for people with a disability, especially people from diverse backgrounds. Even women's rights were right up there on the agenda for organizations and the community to start addressing. But it would be another 20 years before gay rights would get an equal footing here in Australia.

So, during the era while this was unfolding, I was coming to terms with my disability, my childhood upbringing, my search for my natural mother, and my denial of my Italian background, as well as my sexuality. Being a feminist was the easy part for me. Being short-statured made me stand out wherever I went and I had very low self-esteem and negative body image at the time. However, I had some great friends around me who supported me through some very tough times and encouraged me to explore all parts of myself.

So I enrolled in counselling to assist me with coming to terms with my poor body image and dealing with my abandonment at birth by my mother. This also impacted on my feeling that she left me because I was born with short stature. Then the journey of exploring my sexuality could finally be enjoyed, as I had no barriers to hinder my journey.

So, one night, a friend took me out for dinner and then we went to a night club after that. I remember this night so well because I can clearly visualize myself sitting at the bar watching people of the same sex dancing together. The club was a gay bar and I instantly felt at home. It felt so right to be there. It was like I was coming home. It would be sometime later that I would end up in a lesbian relationship and come out. However, there was no going back…

So, coming out… what was it like?

I guess in my life that coming out as a feminist, being short-statured, holding political positions, etc., was easier than coming out as a lesbian. Why? I think this is because I felt that I had a lot to lose, and I worried about what people would say and how they would react. Homosexuality and gay rights have only just started to really be accepted here in Australia.

I remember coming out to a few people at work when I had my first lesbian relationship in the 1980s. I was advised not to make it public knowledge as it could have an impact on promotional opportunities, etc. People even made comments about the way I dressed and said I was making a statement. To me, I wasn't. I was dressing for comfort. Living a gay life was behind closed doors and discrimination against gay people was everywhere. Some social circles and friends disappeared when they found out. This resulted in me isolating myself for a period of time.

Then I woke up one morning and said to myself that the only way for things to change was to acknowledge all aspects of myself and be proud. In doing so, it would invite other people to do the same.

This was the turning point for me. Accepting myself meant there was a flow-on effect on the people around me. They would comment on how comfortable I was in my skin. And yes, it is okay to be a lesbian; a short-statured person; a person from a migrant background; a strong feminist – and the list goes on. I don't need to keep coming out – I am Out and Proud.

As you can see, there are many diverse labels that others can attach to me. All my life I have worked at threading these wonderful strands of my being into a rich and whole tapestry that is Margherita. I am comfortable in my whole skin. That's what Pride is.

You may call me Margherita.

14
Yenn Purkis

Yenn Purkis is an autistic and non-binary author, advocate, public speaker, government official, and mentor. Their pronouns are they/them. They were diagnosed as autistic when they were 20. They also have a diagnosis of schizophrenia, which they gained when they were 21. Yenn is a very proud autistic, non-binary, asexual, and schizophrenic person. They value and like themselves just as they are and wish that sentiment to all other queer and disabled people. Yenn lives in Canberra, Australia and loves writing, art, and cats.

www.yennpurkis.com

Yenn's story
Reflections of Yenn at 15

Dear fifteen-year-old me,

I am now 48 years old. My life now is very different to the life you know.

I am the author of many books about autism, I give talks all over the world, and people seek me out for my knowledge around disability and gender diversity. I am an out loud and proud autistic and ADHD person with schizophrenia and I am also out loud and proud as a non-binary and asexual person. I like and value myself. I work full time in the Australian Public Service and work the equivalent of two full time jobs. Just like you, I love being active and writing and making art. I have 12 published books with more on the way. I am described as an overachiever! I own a beautiful home in Canberra and am about to get myself a cat. Yes, I still love cats!

I remember what it was like being you. You were always anxious and it seemed like everyone hated you, especially at school. You wanted more than anything to be accepted by your peers but nothing you tried helped you to be socially accepted. There are some things I can tell you about what you are like at age 15. You were extremely accomplished academically. In fact, I now have a Master's degree but have never once studied for an exam or test. Study and academia came so easily but I know you have never recognized that as a positive attribute. I recently learned that my parents described this ability to absorb information on topics I was passionate about as being like osmosis. The information just somehow gets into my brain. At 15 you have had some lovely passionate interests too. I remember your passion for cats, *Doctor Who*, and politics. Like most autistic people you love spending time on your passions. Take pleasure in this where you can.

You probably don't know this but you are actually a very thoughtful, kind, and empathetic person. You are quite different to your peers – and your family. I know that you have a hard time because of this. People think you are just all about study and reading but you also have a very kind heart. You see the best in people and you want good things for the people in your life. Sadly, you have a lot of trouble with bullies. At every school you have attended you have been the most disliked and ostracized kid. I need you to know that this is not your fault. The only people to blame for the bullying are the bullies. One thing I can tell you about bullies is that they usually do it because they feel powerless themselves. If you were to stand up to them, they might back off. But you are such a lovely person that you have never stood up to them. I can tell you that things improve in this space and you will find some amazing friends who love, value, and respect you just the way you are. And if this helps any, research demonstrates that people who bully at school often have some negative outcomes themselves. I know you wouldn't wish misery on anyone but I figure that might provide some perspective.

Socialists and the road to a desperate life

I know you have a passion for politics. You will soon join the International Socialists. You love being a socialist but it gets you in trouble with your family – you are always arguing, especially with your dad. You call your family "petit bourgeois". You even tell your dad he is a waste of space! But the best thing about the socialists is that you have 100 instant adult friends! All you have to do is agree with them and go to a meeting or two and have an opinion about the Russian revolution. You will move away from home at the age of 17 and live with specialist friends. People tell you that you are too young to leave home but you figure you have never been any older so can't see this.

You will be a socialist for another four years. Being a socialist gave you so much certainty. You knew you were right – it was very satisfying. As you got older you started to change your views and doubt yourself more. But as a socialist you have all the answers. After you have been a socialist for a couple of years you developed a passion – not for politics, so much as for aggression. You wanted to be on the receiving end of violence from the police. You would go to protests with the wish to be arrested. You discovered that it is very easy to get in trouble with the law! You were one of the "Richmond Eight" – getting arrested at a violent protest on a picket line. You would actively seek out police attention. This was not a good thing but sadly things got worse – significantly worse!

Crime, drugs, and alcohol

Through the socialists you tried alcohol and marijuana and you liked them. And through the socialists you met "Dave". I will not use his actual name as he was a very scary person. He was a criminal and you actually found that exciting. I feel very remorseful about that time in your life but I also know that Dave took advantage of you. Through knowing Dave and committing crimes with him you ended up in jail. It was terrifying and you felt so guilty about what you did that you were glad you got caught.

You spent six months in jail. While you were there something happened that would end up changing your life, even if you didn't like it at the time. Your parents sent a clinical psychologist to assess you for what was then called Asperger syndrome and is now just called autism. The psychologist said you fulfilled all the criteria for a diagnosis of Asperger syndrome. This piece of information explained pretty much everything you had experienced in life up to that point. Sadly, it took you another seven years to accept the diagnosis. You thought autism was shameful and that it validated the taunts of the bullies at school. Even while you denied your autism, deep down you knew it was correct. But it was very raw and personal. Interestingly, when you started to like yourself was the point at which you were happy to accept your autism. You now talk about autism all over the world and write books about it. You are one of the most visible autistic advocates in the world. It just took a little while to get to that point of pride.

Mental illness

In addition to your autism, you have a mental illness – well, a few of them to be correct. After you were released from prison when you were 20, you used a lot of drugs. This was because the experience of prison was traumatic and you were doing what is often called self-medicating. Drugs and being high were a passion for you, just like *Doctor Who* and cats had been when you were young. Autistic people often have passions and usually this is a positive thing. But for you this particular passion was damaging. You became homeless and the stress of this combined with the drug use resulted in you becoming psychotic. You ended up in hospital – the first of a large number of admissions for mental health reasons over the past 30 years or so. If I were to give you one piece of advice from the place in hindsight, it would probably be to keep away from drugs. It took you several years – and many more hospital admissions and prison stays – for you to realize that drugs were not a good thing. I have now been clean and sober for almost 20 years and it is a good thing. However, I still have the mental illness – which goes by the name of schizophrenia – and I suspect I will have it for the rest of my life. I wish I had known this when I was your age.

Journey to success

When you were 25 you took a decision to be what you called "ordinary". That sounds absolutely horrible but in fact it was a good thing. You decided that you would have an education, a mortgage, a professional job, and a suit – maybe not in that order! You enrolled in art school so that you could get a degree. This was only one year after you were released from prison for the last time. You went through a period of time where you could have gone one way or the other in terms of your life direction. Thankfully the good decisions outweighed the poor ones and you built your experience and confidence around things like work and education.

In 2005 something happened which would change your life in a big way. You wrote a book. The reason for this was that an autistic mentor you had at the time had encouraged you to write your life story. Her name was Polly Samuel and unlike the criminal Dave who had been a catalyst in destroying your life, Polly was the opposite. She changed your world for the better. Best of all, Polly taught you about autistic pride.

At the time you met Polly, people had been telling you to write your life story. You kept saying no, thinking that your life story was pretty shameful and publishing it would just give people the opportunity to criticize and blame you! Polly said that if you wrote your story it would be for the parents of autistic kids who were in trouble with the police. Of course, you realized that this was YOUR parents and so you wrote it. It took four weeks to write, two to edit, and three weeks for the first publisher who received the manuscript to agree to publish it!

The book was a huge catalyst for change in your life. You were so excited to be published that you told everyone you knew about it! It gave you immense amounts of joy and confidence. Being a published author was a big deal. Three months after the book came out you applied for two professional jobs in the public service. Without the book I suspect you would not have done this. You were successful in one of your applications and went on to start a new life. And just as an aside, nobody has ever made judgemental comments about your life story. That one Yenn book has now become 12 published books and you have a reputation as being one of the most visible autistic advocates in the world. And I would say to you please be extra nice to Polly when you meet her. Using the benefit of hindsight, I can say that I took Polly for granted a bit which wasn't OK.

You moved to Canberra in 2007 and took up a job in the public service. This was an amazing thing. You did have to answer a lot of questions about your criminal history but the department was convinced that you were not a risk. At the time of writing this letter you have been a public servant for 16 years. You have been promoted twice and you love your job. Your job makes you a bit of an anomaly. You are an autistic ex-prisoner with schizophrenia and a bunch of other mental health issues. And you are an exemplary public servant. You have a great work ethic and take pride in what you do. Your autistic qualities of attention to detail, pattern recognition, and having a low tolerance to errors make you a dream employee. And strangely enough, your criminal history is something of a positive in that you are absolutely fine with hierarchies – and the public service can be seen as a hierarchical employer, with many levels of management and expectations around communicating with people at the various levels.

Unlikely and an anomaly

Recently I did a calculation – you know how much we like lists and inventories! I calculated how long I have been in institutional care – hospital, prison, and residential mental health services. I am now 48 and the amount of my life spent in institutions is (currently) just under ten years. I have spent over 20 per cent of my life in institutions. The amazing thing is that at the time of writing this, I have no wish to be in institutional care. Most people I know with my kind of history really struggle to break free from the grip of the institution but I actively dislike institutions. If I am unwell with psychosis or depression, I will always opt to stay at home and don't go to hospital if I can avoid it. I have no nostalgia for institutions – even the nice ones! This is one of my interesting and unusual attributes.

I take a medication called clozapine. It is sort of the last line of defence drug for schizophrenia. It has potentially dangerous side effects so I need to be monitored on it and have regular appointments with the clozapine nurse. My previous clozapine nurse, a lovely fellow called Ian, said I was "an anomaly" among people with schizophrenia. I don't have many of the usual side effects from the medication and I have a LOT of insight. Very few people with schizophrenia have insight into the illness. The funny thing about this is that I am a small percentage in many things – motivation, ability to manage my illness, not to mention all my various accomplishments. I simply should not be, but I am. And I suspect that all that misery and drama you are about to embark on has some kind of connection to me being unlikely and an anomaly. So maybe keep that in mind when your life is being difficult!

Gender expression

I want to tell you about something called gender diversity. When you are in your early forties you discover a thing called non-binary gender. You know how you have never felt like a girl? How the way you feel about your gender is quite ambiguous? Well, there is a reason for that. You have a gender identity different to the one you were given at birth. You know how you have always felt like your gender was a sort of third option? The good news is that your gender IS a third option. And the even better news is that there are LOADS of other people who have diverse genders.

I am delighted to inform you that there are thousands of different gender identities. I tend to think there are as many gender identities as there are humans on this planet. As a non-binary person, I am able to express my gender in any way that I want. I love being non-binary. It is a total liberation. Sadly, there is a lot of bigotry about gender diversity. While there are many great people and organizations supporting those of us who are trans and gender divergent there are also people that would attack and hate us. These days I am an advocate and one of the areas I am passionate about is gender advocacy. I always say that we cannot be complacent about activism and advocacy. If we don't keep working for inclusion, acceptance, and respect then things will no doubt just get worse.

An advocate

These days I am primarily known as an advocate for disability and gender diversity rights. I do loads of things that help people. When I got out of prison for the last time in 2000, I decided that a new millennium should equal a new life. I also wanted to put as much distance as possible between my criminal history and the present time. I am now heading toward 24 years of not being a prisoner and doing well. I also wanted to change the world and took on an approach to life that people should leave the world in a better place when they depart it than it was when they arrived. I actually think I have done that. If I were to die today, I would have already left a legacy. This kind of thinking is a bit addictive and I am constantly trying to change the world! Sometimes I succeed and other times I just dish out unwanted advice. But mostly it is a good thing!

Identity – Autistic pride, queer pride

These days I have a very strong sense of identity and belong to a huge number of diversity/intersectional groups. I am autistic and ADHD, have a number of mental illness conditions, have a history of institutionalization and incarceration, and am non-binary and asexual. I have a history of poverty and homelessness. Despite – or maybe because of – these "labels" I am a very successful person. I also think my belonging to all of these groups makes me a kinder and more empathetic person. I would love to tell you what to do and what not to do to avoid trauma and poor choices. But I suspect that the reason I am the advocate and author I am now is largely due to all the trauma that you faced over the next few years. I would say avoid violence – both from yourself and others – as it is not a solution to anything. Violence traumatizes you and others. I would also say that you are amazing. You are insightful, kind, intelligent, creative, and ethical. These days people tell me those things all the time – an occupational hazard of having a public profile as a queer and disabled person. However, at your age of 15, you rarely hear anything positive about yourself, which feeds into your lack of confidence and low self-esteem. Bullies are not a source of insight into who you are. I know you hate being an academic and feel it contributes to misery at the hands of bullies. But actually being academic is wonderful. You do not realize how remarkable that is. In fact, you don't realize how remarkable are the many ways in which you will eventually learn but I wish you had learned quicker. You have survived hatred, violence, and trauma and are still full of love, kindness, and the capacity to forgive. This is a rare thing.

I am someone so often victimized, someone who went through hell in prison and suffered homelessness. But I am also someone who holds no blame or hatred. The autobiography you write when you are 30 is unusual in that there is no blame. You are genuinely kind and this impacts on your advocacy. And now, approaching 50, I end up liking myself, having good and genuine friends and being able to share my understanding and experience with others. This is a wonderful outcome.

One last thing

I have one thing to tell you – and every other queer and disabled young person. That is that it will be OK. It changes, it really does. It may not get "fixed" but it will not be the same forever. You will grow and learn. Just hold that tight in your heart. It will change and it will be OK.

15
Summary

There are a number of common threads within the stories in this book. These include:

- Challenging the status quo;
- Advocacy;
- The value of allies and supporters, whoever they may be;
- Experiencing bigotry – transphobia, homophobia, and ableism;
- Bullying;
- Accomplishments;
- Facing and challenging adversity;
- A passion for inclusion;
- Drive and determination;
- Great strengths;
- Life as a journey of growth and discovery;
- Coming out – many different experiences but similarities as well;
- Self-doubt;
- Finding social connections; and
- Discovering and embracing identity.

The stories demonstrate the challenges and also the great strengths that can come with being queer and disabled. They illustrate the need for advocacy, allyship, and the importance of loving and valuing yourself, whoever you may be. The stories are at times very difficult to read given all the discrimination, bullying, and bigotry that the authors have experienced but they are also empowering and positive and demonstrate the power and strength of the authors.

Queer and Disabled identities are absolutely valid and deserving of respect, kindness, and understanding.

The authors hope you have found this book helpful. Sharing our stories helps people to understand queer and disabled identities and brings together some shared experiences. These stories need to be shared. Sharing our stories helps everyone. It helps to address fears as well as hate, bigotry, and bias. It helps others understand what we have experienced and to see things from a different perspective. As humans we communicate through sharing stories. These stories of queer and disabled experience shed a light on our lives and aim to help make the world a more inclusive and respectful place. We are privileged to share our stories with you and to help you understand our experiences and perspective.

Be it about coming out to family, treatment in health care settings, the value of friends and allies, or overcoming bigotry and hate, and many other things, these stories aim to educate and include, to share and affirm.

Notes

1. A niche term of endearment referring to fellow male gays/ queers, resulting in both the feminization and familialization of queer communities.

Suggested discussion topics

- What are some examples of discrimination as experienced by queer and disabled people?
- How can discrimination against queer and disabled people be addressed?
- In what ways can the telling of queer and disabled stories help to advance inclusive places?
- In what ways can allies support the social inclusion of queer and disabled people?

References

Carey, M. and Warren, D. (1999). Mariah Carey - Can't Take That Away (Mariah's Theme). [YouTube video] Available at: www.youtube.com/watch?v=ygO9-_lHsuw [Accessed 22 January 2024].

Darlington Statement. (2017). Darlington Statement. [Online] Available at: https://darlington.org.au/statement/ [Accessed 11 August 2023].

Disability Discrimination Victorian Equal Opportunity and Human Rights Commission. (2023). Disability. [Online] Available at: www.humanrights.vic.gov.au/for-individuals/disability/ [Accessed 11 August 2023].

Fiske, S. T. and Neuberg, S. L. (1990). A continuum of impression formation, from category-based to individuating processes: Influences of information and motivation on attention and interpretation. In: M. P. Zanna, ed., *Advances in Experimental Social Psychology*. San Diego, CA: Academic Press, 1.

Herbert, W. and TEDxCanberra (2017). Anecdotes of a disabled gay. [YouTube video] Available at: www.youtube.com/watch?v=v241teCRl2c&t=58s [Accessed 12 August 2023].

McLaughlin, K. (2014). Are We Willing to Change Our Impression of First Impressions? *Advances in Health Sciences Education: Theory and Practice*, 19(3): 429–431.

Melbourne University. (2023). How to be a good LGBTIQA+ ally. [Online] Available at: https://about.unimelb.edu.au/news-resources/pride-in-action-ally-network/how-to-be-a-good-LGBTIQA-ally [Accessed 11 August 2023].

Muriel's Wedding. (1994). Australia: P. J. Hogan.

People With Disability Australia. (2023). Social model of disability. [Online] Available at: https://pwd.org.au/resources/models-of-disability [Accessed 11 August 2023].

Pink. (2021). All I know so far. [Single] New York: RCA Records.

Pratchett, T. (2013). *Witches Abroad*. London: Corgi Publishing.

Schechner, R. (2013). *Performance Studies: An Introduction*. Third Edition. London and New York: Routledge.

Recommended further reading

Dale, L. K. (2019). *Uncomfortable Labels: My Life as a Gay Autistic Trans*. London: Jessica Kingsley Publishers.

Lawson, W. and Lawson, B. (2017). *Transitioning Together: One Couple's Journey of Gender and Identity Discovery*. London: Jessica Kingsley Publishers.

Marsden, M. (2018). *Queerstories: Reflections on Lives Well Lived from Some of Australia's Finest LGBTQIA+ Writers*. Sydney: Hachette Australia.

Purkis, Y. and Lawson, W. (2021). *The Autistic Trans Guide to Life*. London: Jessica Kingsley Publishers.

Sparrow, M. (2020). *Spectrums: Autistic Transgender People in Their Own Words*. London: Jessica Kingsley Publishers.

Symington, S. (2021). *Coming Out Again: Transition Stories*. London: Jessica Kingsley Publishers.

Index

ableism 38, 77, 79, 95–96

   in friends 47

   internalized 99

   in society 52

abuse 25, 68, 72, 113, 115

   emotional 24

   physical 2, 24

ACT Government Disability Reference Group 13

activism 4–5, 111, 117, 141

adenomyosis 45, 52

advocacy 5, 18, 40, 46, 52, 126, 141, 143

   career in 112

   need for 145

AFAB *see* assigned female at birth

AIDS 76

Ainslee Hooper Consulting 95

alcohol 32, 76, 136

allies 10, 148

AMAB *see* assigned male at birth

animal rights 49

anthropology 95–96, 98–99, 101, 108

anxiety 9, 21, 45, 64, 79, 116

aroha 79

art 33, 48, 67, 70, 81, 92, 133, 138

assigned female at birth (AFAB) 2, 107

assigned male at birth (AMAB) 2

audience 14, 26, 30–31, 67, 71–72

Australasian Autism Research Council (AARC) 56

Australian Public Service 134

authenticity 90, 115

autism, 3, 9, 45, 55–56, 62, 77, 79, 81, 89, 133

   diagnosis 91, 98, 136

   Monotropic theory of 55

   needs 91

   pride 142

BDM *see* Births Deaths and Marriages

behaviours 29, 39, 85

bigotry 2, 7, 141, 146

bipolar disorder 45–46

Births Deaths and Marriages (BDM) 123

body language 65

bullying 24, 97, 135, 146

Cain, John 125
CALD *see* culturally and linguistically diverse
career barriers 77
Carey, Mariah 15
Christian theology 59
chronic headaches 98
chronic pain 45–47
cisgender 2
clozapine 140
Commonwealth Employment Service 125
Commonwealth Rehabilitation Service (CRS) 125
communication 47, 63, 90
   barriers to 91
community xii, 21, 45
   building 111
   rainbow 22
   of weirdos 43
compassion 76, 79–80
confusion 56, 60, 79
consumer representative 127
continuum model 28–29, 32, 34
coping mechanism 99
Crenshaw, Kimberley 7
crime 136

criminal justice system 7,
cultural studies 29
culturally and linguistically diverse (CALD) 117
culture, discovering 129

dance 70
   interpenetrating depictions of 27
   studies 27–29, 33
Dandelion Heart 35
Darlington Statement for Intersex rights 10
depression 113, 140
disability 1, 3, 23, 45, 49, 82, 95, 98–99, 126, 142
   in Australia 15
   community 75–76
   discrimination 5, 20
   dynamic 67
   employment xiv, 97
   and gender diversity 133
   and identities 3
   inclusion 98
   lesbian with 117
   physical 98
   queer with 111
   recruitment programme 126
   and shame 99
   social and medical models of 4

Disability Action Plan 126–127

Disability Justice Plan 35

disabled

    body 34, 40

    identities 5, 7

    movement 27

    person 8, 95, 99

discrimination 14, 125, 146

    disability 5, 20

diversity 8, 23, 132

Diversity Council of Australia 126

drugs 136–137

dwarfism 118, 124

dyscalculia 60

dyslexia 3, 60, 120

dyspraxia 3, 60

education 17, 113–114, 125, 138

embarrassment 49

emotions 49, 61, 116, 121

employment 124

empowerment 7

environment 49

equality 18, 25,

equity 18, 25

Eyrie, Empress 67

family

    discovering 122

environment 121

fashion choices 31

fatigue 46

feminism 113

fibromyalgia 45, 52

fluidity 114

freedom machines 52

friendships 87, 93

    ableist 47

    genuine 70

    romantic 61

gay 8–9, 21, 28, 30, 49, 75–76, 131

    culture 21

    rights 132

gender 41, 49

    advocacy 141

    divergent 3

    diverse artists 111

    diversity 133, 141–142

    expression 141

    identities 141

    stereotypes 107

    studies 113

Goodall, Emma 75

grey-asexual 114

grief 52, 78, 115

harassment 24

headaches 58

health care settings 146

Herbert, Wayne 13

Heslop, Muriel 22

Hinch 123

homelessness 137, 143

homophobia 19–20, 24–25

homosexuality 132

identity 42, 124, 142

   creating 129

   disability and 3

impression formation 28

incarceration 142

inclusion 4, 9–10, 17–18, 23, 96, 100, 112

inclusive environment 112

individuals, narrative experiences of 30

informed opinions 93

inspiration porn 5

institutional care 119

institutional environment 119

institutionalization 142

institutions 91

intelligence 38

International Day for People with Disability 8

intersectional

communities/groups 6, 127

   identity 31

intersex 2

   human rights movement 11

journalism 46, 51

journey 20, 56, 87, 96, 101, 106, 114–116, 131, 138

Kennett, Jeff 125

kindness 80

kinetic cue 32

Kirner, Joan 125

knowledge

   access to 57

   facilitator of 102

leadership 16, 111

learning difficulty 60

lesbian 75, 78, 81, 86, 117, 130–132

LGBTQIA+ xi–1, 6–7, 13–14, 25, 35, 81, 117

lived experiences 112

logic 93

love 50, 71

management 140

marriage equality 21

masculinity, Asian forms of 31

masking 47

memory 57, 119

mental health 45, 55, 137

mental illness 48, 137

micro-aggressions 5

MIECAT 81

militarization, critiques of 104

military service 104

mimic 106

mobility 33

   aids 67

music 48, 70

National Ethnic Disability Alliance
   128

neurodivergence 3–4, 7, 40, 56,
   116

   community 77

   research 55

neurotypical 3

opinions 93

osteomyelitis 57

parental ideology 59

patient care 82

performance 29, 32, 70, 72

performance studies 30

philosophy 51

physical education 58

physical efforts 103

Pinney, Freya 81

poetry 46

political act 7

political organizations 88

political performance artist 111

popular culture 101

popular media 79

poverty 7

Pratchett, Terry 71

privilege 11, 18

pronouns 2

psychosis 140

public service 139

queer 1, 30, 45, 78

   community 75–76

   and disability 111

   drag performer 31

   experience 10

   identities 1, 42

   pride 142

   role in society 10

   theory 113

racial identity 114

rag trade 118

recognition 16, 56

relationships 47, 85–86
    healthy and unhealthy 77
representation 9
resilience 40, 115–116
Ringwald, Molly 101
romantic identity 41
Royal Children's Hospital 120

Schechner, Richard 30
schizophrenia 139–140
    diagnosis of 133
self-acceptance 116
self-care needs 92
self-confidence 35
self-discovery 112
self-expression 41
self-worth 80
sensory sensitivities 92
sexual identity 41
sexual intercourse 6
sexual preference 85
sexuality 49, 61, 75–76, 82, 85,
    114, 131
    in adolescence 86
    perceptions of 86
"Silent Tears" exhibition 128
skills 17, 19, 77, 106
social clubs 88

social engagements, structured
    88
social identity, constriction of 88
social justice 23, 49
social media groups 88
social model of disability 4
social situations 87
socialization 47
socialists 135
societal expectations 114
somatic experiencing 92
spectator 30
speech patterns 39
stereotypes 9, 28–29, 31
    gender 107
stigma 14
stimming 41
structured outlines 65
stupidity 38
success 49
    journey to 138
survival 40
Sydney Gay and Lesbian Mardi
    Gras 8
systemic discrimination 125

talents 19
Tease-Able Burlesque School 67
TEDx talk 29–30, 32

teenager 60, 64, 70, 77, 97

transgender 2, 10

trauma 24, 72, 115

Vincent, Kelly 35

violence 19, 24, 128, 143

virginity 86

visual cue 32

walk, distinct features of 33

weirdness 43

wheelchair 4, 37–38

Witches Abroad (Pratchett) 71

women

   equality movement 96

   rights 130

World Dwarf Games 128

Young, Stella 5, 14

www.ingramcontent.com/pod-product-compliance
Lightning Source LLC
Chambersburg PA
CBHW070341270326
41926CB00017B/3938